VeggieTales

VeggieConnections

Connecting to a Powerful Relationship with God.

Family
DEVOTIONAL

by Cindy Kenney
and Doug Peterson

www.bigidea.com

INTEGRITY®
PUBLISHERS
family

www.integritypublishers.com

Based on the VeggieConnections curriculum developed by Cindy Kenney

VeggieConnections Family Devotional
ISBN: 1-59145-261-9
Copyright © 2005 by Big Idea, Inc.
Illustrations copyright © 2005 by Big Idea, Inc.

Requests for information should be addressed to:
Integrity Publishers, 5250 Virginia Way, Suite 110, Brentwood, TN 37027

_____

Written by: Cindy Kenney and Doug Peterson
Editor: Cindy Kenney
Art Direction: John Trent
Layout and Design: Blum Graphic Design, Big Idea Design

ACKY PROBLEMS

Tell everyone to create some *wacky* problems. Talk (and laugh) about your wacky problems, then celebrate how

God helps us to overcome *real* problems.

Wacky ideas: wear socks on your hands; wear your shirt backward and pajamas on your head; tie your shoelaces together with someone else's. Set the table with plates upside down and silly utensils to use as silverware.

CUCUMBER CONNECTION

• Have you ever not asked for help when you needed it?

• What has been the biggest problem you've ever gotten into?

• Write down three things you can do to overcome a problem. Talk about your ideas with the entire family.

THINK-LINK-ACT

THINK about the problems that you have right now. Then think about the problems that other people you know may have.

LINK what you know about God's help to your problems. One way God helps is to send others to help.

ACT on it by asking God if there is anyone you can help right now.

lift up my eyes to the hills—where does my help come from? My help comes from the LORD, the Maker of heaven and earth" (Psalm 121:1–2). Even when we're tangled up in problems, you help us, Lord. Thank you.

Devotional – 16

WINGS

Long ago, Snoodles didn't know they could fly. Until one day, a little Snoodle fell from a biggle-bag tree! But before he hit the ground, his wings fluttered, and he rose in the air like a blue-crested Bing!

Toodle-loo flew through Snoodleburg! He dipped and he dove, and he shouted out loud, "I can fly! So can you!"

But the people of Snoodleburg didn't believe him. They thought Toodle-loo was just plain odd. So Toodle-loo's friends told him not to tell anyone about flying. "People will like you better if you just stop flying!"

But Toodle-loo couldn't keep this wonderful thing to himself. He wanted everyone to enjoy this gift that their Creator had given them.

*So the boy spent a year racing high in
    the sky
Until they finally believed ALL
    Snoodles could fly.
The Snoodles discovered what
    wings were there for.
The Creator had made them so each
    one could soar!*

EARN HOW TO FLY!

Zoodle-loo wanted all the Snoodles to know the good news that they could fly!
We have good news to share too! We get to tell others how much Jesus loves them.
Paul knew all about this. That's why he went all over the world telling everyone
about Jesus.

WHAT DOES THE BIBLE SAY?

Acts 9:20-31

Paul wanted everyone to learn about Jesus!

When he had been known as Saul, he hated Christians. He was mean to them and put them in jail. But after he came to know Jesus, he changed! Saul changed so much that he promised to do anything to help others learn about Jesus.

So Saul changed his name to Paul. Then he learned all he could about God and his Son, Jesus.

But some people said, "Wasn't he the one who was throwing Christians in jail and killing us?"

Plus, the religious leaders he worked with as Saul became so angry with him that they wanted Paul killed.

Paul's new Christian followers, helped to watch over him and keep him safe. They helped him to escape people who wanted to kill him by lowering him over a city wall. Finally, when Paul arrived in Jerusalem, he continued to spread the news of Jesus across the world!

The good news flew from country to country—as if it had wings.

BIBLE FACT:

Paul started out as a student. Then he became a preacher, but he also had a job as a tent maker.

Family Fun Connection:
IF YOU COULD FLY

Let your ideas take flight! Challenge everyone in your family to draw a picture of him - or herself with wings. Then think: *If you could fly, where would you fly to spread God's news?*

After you share your ideas with one another, fold the paper into paper airplanes and see how far you can get your plane to fly!

CUCUMBER CONNECTION

- What is God's good news?
- Why is the good news something to get excited about?
- How can you spread the good news around—as if it had wings?

THINK-LINK-ACT

THINK about the people you know who may not know about Jesus.

LINK the people who don't know Jesus to your family and friends who do love Jesus.

ACT on it by inviting them to church worship or some fun gatherings with your Christian friends.

"How beautiful on the mountains are the feet of those who bring good news" (Isaiah 52:7). Jesus, let us be your messengers. Help us to spread your message.

PART THREE

THE LOVE CONNECTION

CONNECTING TO LOVE THROUGH JESUS

The Love Connection Verse

"'Love the Lord your God with all your heart and with all your soul and with all your mind.' This is the first and greatest commandment. And the second is like it: 'Love your neighbor as yourself.'" (Matthew 22:37–39)

WELCOME TO FLIBBER-O-LOO

High in the hills, past the rocks and the rubble, were two tiny towns that were nothing but trouble.

One of the towns was Flibber-o-loo, where the women and men, since seventeen-ten, have worn on their heads one big shoe. The other town was Jibberty-lot, where people wear on their heads—a big pot.

My name is Junior Asparagus, and I live in Jibberty-lot, so I wear a pot on my head. The two towns constantly fought with each other. Day and night, people threw shoes and pots at each other—that is, until they learned an important lesson.

I was the first person to learn that important lesson, so I love the people of Flibber-o-loo, even though they wear shoes on their heads. (Have you heard of anything sillier?) As soon as I learned that lesson, I tried to share it with my fellow Jibberty-lot neighbors and then we shared it with the Flibbians too!

In the next eight devotionals, hopefully you'll learn to love both the Flibbians and the people of Jibberty-lot.

We're also going to learn from Jesus how to love our neighbors, even if we think they're strange or mean. (By "neighbors," we're talking about the people we meet every day, and the people we know are our neighbors in the next town or state or even country!)

Jesus is God, and God is love. So there's no better teacher than him.

GOD IS LOVE

THE PARABLE OF THE LOVING KING

There was a new king! Unlike so many other kings, this king was good, kind, and loved his kingdom like they were his children.

To celebrate, the king sent out invitations to all the people in Flibber-o-loo and Jibberty-lot, inviting them to a party.

Most of the people were overjoyed! But not all the people liked the new king.

"He's going to be trouble," some said. "He thinks he's better than us," said others.

They refused to go. This made the king very sad.

Still, his party was fabulous! Those who attended discovered that he was a truly wonderful king. In return for coming to his party, the king presented each guest with a beautiful new shoe or pot for his or her head—so magnificent—that it felt like they were each getting a crown!

Each guest came to the party feeling very average, but each one of them left feeling like a prince or princess!

BORN TWICE!

God loves us so much that he invites us to be his sons and daughters. He wants us to be a prince or princess in his kingdom.

Jesus invited many people to enter his kingdom. But not everyone accepted the invitation. Nicodemus was one of the smart ones.

WHAT DOES THE BIBLE SAY?

John 3:1-21

Nicodemus was a Pharisee—a Jewish teacher. Many Pharisees didn't like Jesus, but not Nicodemus. He'd heard Jesus teach, and he was bursting with questions.

Nicodemus was afraid the other Pharisees would get mad at him for seeing Jesus. So he sneaked over at night to the house where Jesus was staying.

Jesus told Nicodemus, "No one can see God's kingdom without being born again."

This baffled Nicodemus. "How can I be born when I'm old? I can't go back inside my mother!"

But Jesus said that being "born again" is a second birth, and that we are made new as we begin a brand-new life with God.

Then Jesus spoke some of the most important words in the whole Bible: "God so loved the world that he gave his one and only Son, that whoever believes in him shall not perish but have eternal life."

Jesus wanted everyone to know that if we believe in Jesus, we are invited to his forever party! When we accept his invitation, we will be made new!

Instead of receiving a brand-new boot or shoe that feels like a crown, we get a crown of eternal life, which means we are invited to be a member of God's kingdom forever!

BIBLE FACT:

Nicodemus was a Pharisee who was a member of a larger religious ruling council called the Sanhedrin in Jerusalem. The concept of being born again was brand-new and unlike anything the religious leaders had ever heard of.

NGDOM PARTY

Have your own kingdom party!
Celebrate Jesus as king! Play royal
games, eat majestic food, and make

crowns that say, "God is love!" Then
crown each participant as a child
of God.

CUCUMBER CONNECTION

- The Bible says that God is love. What does that mean?
- Why did God send Jesus into the world?
- What does it mean to have eternal life?

THINK-LINK-ACT

THINK about a time when you may not have felt loved.

LINK that to Jesus' invitation for you to follow him.

ACT on it by accepting Jesus' invitation. You can be a prince or princess in God's kingdom!

his is how God showed his love among us: He sent his one and only
on into the world that we might live through him" (1 John 4:9).
oving King, thank you for inviting us into your kingdom!

I HAVE JESUS AS MY SAVIOR AND COUNSELOR

Devotional – 18

THE PARABLE OF THE CLIFF-HANGER

Once upon a time, a sheep tumbled off of a cliff right between the towns of Flibber-o-loo and Jibberty-lot. The poor sheep clung to a branch for dear life.

Within moments, emergency crews from both cities arrived. But they started arguing about the best way to save him.

"Let's use a long shoelace to pull the sheep up," said the Mayor of Flibber-o-loo.

"That's crazy!" said the Mayor of Jibberty-lot. "We should lower a pot for the sheep to be let down in."

"A shoelace!"

"A pot!"

"A shoelace!"

While the two mayors bickered, no one noticed as a simple shepherd rescued the sheep. But he didn't use a shoelace. And he didn't use a pot. The shepherd climbed down HIMSELF and carried the sheep to safety.

Shoelaces break and pots wobble. But a shepherd's love is strong and steady.

HE SPIRIT AND THE SAVIOR

One of the names for Jesus is the Good Shepherd. He loves us so much that he came down from heaven to watch over his flock and save us—just like the shepherd who climbed down to save the sheep.

But Jesus also knew we would need someone to be with us when he left this world. That's why he gave us the gift of the Holy Spirit.

WHAT DOES THE BIBLE SAY?

John 16:5-15

During the Last Supper, before Jesus died on the cross, Jesus told his disciples that he was going someplace where they could not follow.

Jesus knew that when he was gone from this world, his friends would be sad and lonely. So Jesus promised that when he was gone, he would send his Holy Spirit. We can't see the Holy Spirit, but the Spirit lives inside of our hearts.

Jesus called the Holy Spirit the "Counselor," which is like a helper.

He explained that the Spirit shows us right from wrong. The Spirit gives us wisdom when we face tough decisions. And the Spirit helps us understand God's Word.

People who have jobs as counselors do many of the same things. They listen to troubles. They help people to make right choices. They help to show people right from wrong.

But the Holy Spirit is a Counselor like no other, because he always has the right answer, and he is ready to listen any time of the day.

BLE FACT:

The dove is one of the symbols for the Holy Spirit. When John the Baptist baptized Jesus, the Spirit came down on Jesus like a dove.

CREATE A WIND SOCK!

Write "GOD LOVES (insert name)" on a large piece of construction paper or poster-board. Decorate as desired. Roll it into a tube shape with a two-inch overlap and tape solidly in place. Attach a string to the top for hanging, and fasten ribbons, crepe paper, or strips of tissue paper to the inside bottom of the sock so that the strips can dangle in the wind. Staple or tape in place.

Watch the wind blow through it and flutter the dangling bottom. Like the wind, the Ho... Spirit is invisible too, working through us to counsel and lift us up when we're feeling down. Hang it outdoors as a reminder that with the Holy Spirit, you, too, can soar!

CUCUMBER CONNECTION

• How can Jesus save us from our sins?

• Who is the Holy Spirit?

• How can the Holy Spirit help us every day?

THINK-LINK-ACT

THINK about how important it is for you to make good decisions and choices.

LINK those needs to how the Holy Spirit is available to you to help you make the right choices anytime and anywhere

ACT on it by leaning on the Holy Spirit's help. Pray for help from the Holy Spirit; that he may guide you in making these choices.

"[May he] strengthen you with power through his Spirit in your inner being" (Ephesians 3:16b). Jesus, thank you for sending your Holy Spirit as our comfort and guide.

I HAVE JESUS TO TEACH ME HOW TO LOVE

THE PUDDING PARABLE

The doctor from Flibber-o-loo decided to build a big, fancy house—a house that would make people go, "Oooooooooh!" and love her a lot!

So the doctor built her house on a hill made of chocolate pudding! It was so amazing that the doctor could stick her spoon right out the window to scoop up some pudding anytime she was hungry.

Best of all, people walked by and said, "Oooooooooh!" They had never seen a house built out of chocolate pudding before. That made the doc pleased as pudding, and she felt more loved.

Until it rained.

The rain melted the pudding. So when the wind blew, the house fell down with a loud SPLAT!

"Oooooooooh!" said the people.

The next day, the doctor moved in with her sister, Bertha. Bertha's house wasn't fancy, and no one said, "Oooooooooh!"

But it was built on a rock. And Bertha loved her sister.

ACTION ATTITUDES

In the Bible, Jesus said that if you follow his teaching, you'll be as wise as a person who built his house on solid rock (Matthew 7:24–29). Jesus taught us many important things. One of his very special teachings is called the Sermon on the Mount, where Jesus taught us something called the "Beatitudes."

WHAT DOES THE BIBLE SAY?

Matthew 5:1-12

Jesus wanted to teach us about the kind of action-attitudes that would please God and bring us eternal happiness. Our attitudes and actions are important to God, because they show God and others the truth about who we are and are willing to be. That's why they're called the "BEatitudes."

Jesus began each one with the word "blessed," which means happy, praiseworthy, and wonderful. To be blessed means we can receive special joy that comes only from God. The Beatitudes are a guideline for how we can live our lives in faith to God:

1. Blessed are those who know they need God.

2. Blessed are those who are comforted by God when they're sad.

3. Blessed are those who don't think too highly of themselves.

4. Blessed are those who hunger for what is right.

5. Blessed are those who are kind and forgiving to others.

6. Blessed are those who have clean hearts.

7. Blessed are those who make peace with others.

8. Blessed are those who follow God even when people hurt us for loving him.

No matter what happens, God is always with us—like a rock—a safe and solid foundation that cannot be shaken or moved.

BIBLE FACT:

The Beatitudes are part of the Sermon on the Mount because Jesus taught them on a mountainside near Capernaum. They were taught to very large crowds of people who came to listen to Jesus preach over several day's time.

"PUDDING PICNIC"

Make some chocolate pudding and have a "pudding picnic" in your backyard. While you're outside, look at the foundation of your house or apartment building. Describe how you think it was built, what materials were used, and how the foundation has to be strong or the house will fall. Talk about how God is the foundation that holds up our entire life.

CUCUMBER CONNECTION

• Why did Jesus spend his time teaching the people?

• Why did Jesus teach the Beatitudes?

• Talk about the Beatitudes and how you can work together as a family to grow in these action-attitudes.

THINK-LINK-ACT

THINK about which action-attitudes you struggle with.

LINK those struggles to different ways you can begin to make some changes.

ACT on it by talking it over with your family so they can support you and remind you that God is always present.

esus replied, 'If anyone loves me, he will obey my teaching. My Father will ove him, and we will come to him and make our home with him'" (John 14:23). Thank you, Jesus, for teaching us Beatitudes that show us how to love.

Devotional – 20

THE PARABLE OF ROSES

"Let's win this year's Rose Bowl!" shouted the Jibberty-lot coach to his Flower-Power team. "And don't forget your SAWS!"

At the end of the season, Sarah Diggindot showed the coach how she had sawed off the buds as soon as they appeared. Her pot didn't have any roses.

Neither did Billy Millinot's pot. Billy had tried hammers, screw-drivers, and even pliers to grow his roses. But they hadn't helped at all.

The petals on Alfred Linkalot's roses were withered and brown. He had used a SAW, but he had forgotten one important part! (The last letter!)

Tammy Kindlekot's plant had beautiful roses growing bright and strong. The judge gave it a blue ribbon! Then he praised her for using the SAWS—**S**oil, **A**ir, **W**ater, and **S**unlight—as a constant source of power to grow her roses.

"Ooooh!" said Billy.

"Now I get it," said Sarah.

Because Tammy had faithfully used the SAWS to help her grow roses, she was asked to lead this year's parade!

HE POWER SOURCE

Plants need sunlight, air, soil, and water, or they die. These things are their source of life. In the same way, Jesus is our source of life. He gives us love every day, and together with him, we can blossom and grow.

n the middle of a storm, the disciples found out just how much they needed esus too!

WHAT DOES THE BIBLE SAY?

Matthew 14:22-36

One day, while Jesus was praying, a violent storm swept down on his disciples on the Sea of Galilee. The waves crashed hard against their boat. So Jesus stepped out onto the water and walked across the lake—and did not sink!

The disciples were terrified. "It's a ghost!" they shrieked. But Jesus called, "Don't be afraid. It's me."

Then Peter said, "Lord, if it's really you, tell me to come to you."

"Come," Jesus answered. So Peter stepped onto the water. Keeping his eyes on Jesus, he walked right toward him!

But when Peter took his eyes off Jesus and saw the tall waves, he suddenly became frightened. "Lord! Save me!" he shouted. So Jesus reached out his hand and caught Peter before he sank into the water.

When Peter kept his eyes on Jesus, he trusted him and was able to do amazing things. Jesus was his source of power. But when Peter looked away and gave into his fears, he began to sink.

If we're ever in trouble, look toward Jesus. He is our power source too!

IBLE FACT:

The Sea of Galilee—The Sea of Galilee is actually a lake, but it's a pretty big one. This lake is about twelve and a half miles long and seven and a half miles wide.

USE YOUR "SAWS"

Plant flower seeds in a planter or small pot. Decorate the container as desired. Be sure to use your SAWS: Soil, Air, Water, and Sunlight. Talk to your local garden shop to make sure you care for the flower properly.

Use the plant as a reminder to invite God into your life. Remember, plants need Soil, Air, Water, and Sunlight to grow and live; we need God to grow and live.

CUCUMBER CONNECTION

- What would you do if you saw Jesus walking across a lake at night?
- What are some things you can do to keep your eyes on Jesus?
- When you feel scared like the disciples, what can you do?

THINK-LINK-ACT

THINK about what happens when you take your eyes off God.

LINK that to what happens when you've been tempted to do something wrong.

ACT on it by keeping your eyes on Jesus. Remember that God is your power source. Read your Bible and pray to God every day.

"Dear friends, let us love one another, for love comes from God" (1 John 4:7a). Jesus, help me walk with you every day.

I HAVE JESUS TO SHOW ME HOW TO FORGIVE

THE PARABLE OF THE SHOELACES

The Banker of Flibber-o-loo went to the Cobbler who had borrowed one million shoelaces from him. "I've come for the shoelaces!"

The Cobbler was terrified. He didn't have one million shoelaces! So he begged for forgiveness. "I'm sorry. I don't have them. Please forgive me!"

The Banker decided to show the Cobbler mercy. "I forgive you. You don't have to pay."

The very next day, the Cobbler stamped up to a shoeshine boy and shouted, "You owe me ten shoelaces!"

The shoeshine boy couldn't pay him back. But did the Cobbler forgive him? No! He tried to throw the shoeshine boy into jail.

When the Banker found out, he was furious. "I forgave you for one million shoelaces, but you didn't forgive that boy for only ten."

The Cobbler felt like a heel. But he, too, learned how to forgive others.

So no matter who you are, be sure to forgive. It's good for the sole—and the soul.

JUST ASK!

God is willing to forgive us for anything! All we have to do is ask him. God wants us to forgive others too.

Jesus also told a dramatic tale of forgiveness in the Gospel of Luke. It's called the Prodigal Son.

WHAT DOES THE BIBLE SAY?

Luke 15:11-32

A man had two very different sons. One day, the youngest asked their father for his share of their family's money. The father loved his son, so he gave him the money.

The son took the money, packed his bags, and ran off to spend it. He got a little crazy, had some fun, and wasted every cent. Soon, he didn't have a penny left and found himself hungry and without food.

The son could not find a good job. So when he was offered the chance to feed some smelly, stinky pigs, he agreed to do it. But he received so little money for that, he found himself wishing he could eat the pig's food!

Finally, the son decided to go home. He would ask for his father's forgiveness and ask to be one of his hired workers.

When his father saw him coming, his face lit up. The father was so happy to hear his son ask for forgiveness that he gave his son a robe, a beautiful ring, and new sandals. He even threw a big party.

That's how God forgives us too!

BIBLE FACT:

This Little Piggy—It was against the Jewish/Mosaic Law for the Jews to feed pigs. So the son had to feel pretty lousy to wish he could eat pigs' food!

PUPPET SHOW

Act out the "The Parable of the Shoelaces" as a puppet show. Make sock or paper lunch bags as the puppets. Put shoes on your hands and act out the story from behind a couch, low wall, or cardboard—anything you can use as your puppet theater.

CUCUMBER CONNECTION

• Think about a time you were forgiven. How did you feel?

• Think about a time you forgave someone else? How did you feel?

• Do you need to tell anyone you're sorry right now? Talk about it.

THINK-LINK-ACT

THINK about something you have done wrong or a way in which someone may have done something wrong to you.

LINK what you have learned to someone you may know who has a hard time forgiving.

ACT on it by praying that God will help you to forgive in the future, and that God will help anyone else you know to forgive others too.

orgive us our debts, as we also have forgiven our debtors" (Matthew 6:12).
esus, please help us to forgive others as you so freely forgive us.

I HAVE JESUS TO SHOW ME HOW TO LOVE MY NEIGHBOR

Devotional – 22

THE PARABLE OF FLIBBER-O-LOO

A cucumber from Flibber-o-loo was walking with his blue plastic lobster when some robbers knocked the shoe off of his head, took his milk money, and stuck him upside down in a hole!

Both the Mayor and the Doctor from Flibber-o-loo came by, but both were too dreadfully busy to pull him out of the hole.

Finally, a boy from Jibberty-lot came by. At first, the boy wasn't going to help, because Jibberty-lot and Flibber-o-loo did not get along! But then he remembered that God made all of us special and wants us to treat others the way we want to be treated.

So the boy pulled the cucumber from the hole and took him to Flibber-o-loo to get well.

Everyone learned a lesson after seeing what the boy had done. From that day on, the people in Flibber-o-loo and Jibberty-lot stopped throwing shoes and pots at each other. Instead, they threw candy and flowers to show love to their neighbor.

HO'S MY NEIGHBOR?

oving our neighbors isn't always easy. Sometimes we don't get along. Sometimes we on't understand why they act the way they do. Some neighbors might even wear hoes on their heads when they should know that pots make better headgear!

esus told a similar story in Luke 10. It's one of the most famous parables of all—the arable of the Good Samaritan.

WHAT DOES THE BIBLE SAY?

Luke 10:25-37

Jewish man was walking from erusalem to Jericho when he was uddenly attacked by robbers! They ook everything he had, beat him, nd left him half dead.

little while later, a Jewish teacher ame by, but he chose to ignore im by walking on the other side of he road. Then, another Jewish eader passed, but he, too, ignored he poor man.

hat's when a Samaritan came own the road. Now, it's important o know that Samaritans and Jews not only didn't like each other, but often held very different views. But when the Samaritan saw the hurt Jewish man, he felt compassion for his neighbor.

So the Samaritan took the injured Jew to an inn to recover. He even used his own money to pay for his stay and medical care.

So who was the real neighbor to the hurt Jewish man? Who showed him love? The answer is easy. God wants us to show love to *our* neighbors too!

BLE FACT:

parable is a story that Jesus told to help illustrate a message that od wants us to learn.

A SILLY PARTY

Have a Flibber-o-loo party and invite some neighbors to join you! Wear shoes and pans on your head. Take turns tossing a shoe into a laundry basket and popcorn into a pot.

Race with a shoe balanced on your head. Scoop cotton balls into a pot while blindfolded. End the party with a treasure hunt throughout your entire neighborhood!

CUCUMBER CONNECTION

• If someone was bullied at school, would you come to their rescue? Or would you walk on by or pretend not to see?

• What makes a good neighbor?

• How can you be a better neighbor?

THINK-LINK-ACT

THINK about a neighbor you haven't met or who doesn't know God.

LINK those neighbors to different ways you can show them love and tell them about God.

ACT on it by making specific plans to get to know them and invite them to a church event.

"Whoever loves God must also love his brother" (1 John 4:21b).
Jesus, show me ways to love my neighbor.

votional – 23

HE PARABLE OF THE PICKLE

The King had put the Chief Shoe Freshener n charge of his kingdom while he was away. But instead of polishing the pans and fresh-ning the shoes, he did nothing but play games, paint pictures, toss water balloons, and dance!

The Chief Pan Washer warned the Freshener to return to work. But he didn't listen and was surprised when the King returned early! The Freshener tried to stall the King's wrath by pulling out checkers and playing game after game with the king.

Although he had fun, the King finally went into his palace.

"Wonderful!" said the King, returning outside. The pots are shining, the shoes smell like daisies, and my palace is spotless. You shall be in charge every time I leave!"

The Chief Pan Washer winked. He had done all the work while the King and the Freshener had played checkers.

"I am honored," the Freshener answered. "But I cannot take credit. Please share your reign with the Chief Pan Washer."

The King was very pleased. The Chief Shoe Freshener had done something better than care for the pans and shoes. He had learned to love and respect his fellow workers.

OUR HEART, HIS HOME

In order to have a great relationship with someone, love has to be exchanged between both people. The same is true with having a relationship with Jesus. Jesus loves us completely. So it's important we love him too! The only way we can do that is to connect with him in many ways.

When Jesus left this world, he wanted to do something to show his love for all of us. So he told the disciples how obedience to God would keep us close to him, and he told them how the Holy Spirit would keep him close to us.

WHAT DOES THE BIBLE SAY?

John 14:23-31a

Jesus was going away. Soon, he would be arrested in the Garden of Gethsemene and put on trial. But his disciples didn't know what terrible things were coming. So Jesus wanted to make sure they were ready and remembered what he taught.

"Anyone who loves me will obey my teaching," Jesus told them. "My Father will love him. We will come to him and make our home with him."

What an amazing thing! Jesus said that God, the Creator of the universe, wants to be a part of our lives and live in our hearts forever! That's because Jesus loves us. He wants a relationship with us.

Jesus also told the disciples not to worry when he's gone. "The Father will send a helper to you," he said. "The helper is the Holy Spirit. He will teach you all things. He will remind you of everything I have said to you."

The Holy Spirit was the greatest going-away present ever!

BIBLE FACT:

In John 14, Jesus describes heaven as a wonderful house with many rooms. Jesus is getting a room ready just for us.

POT & PAN RELAY

Have a Pot & Pan Relay.

Fill two large pots with water and put them at one end of the yard. Race to fill two smaller, empty pots at the other end of the yard on the word "go," by dipping cups into the water and carrying them across to the empty ones. Keep filling the empty pots until they overflow. The first team to fill their empty pot wins.

Afterward, talk about how God wants to fill us with his love until we're overflowing—like water.

CUCUMBER CONNECTION

• How does God show his love for us?

• What are some of the ways you can show love to God?

• Why is it important to obey God, even if our parents or teachers aren't looking?

THINK-LINK-ACT

THINK about the people you are supposed to obey.

LINK God's request for us to be obedient to how it can carry over to those people.

ACT on it by showing your obedience to them. (Clean your room, share with a brother or sister, eat healthy, etc.) Show your love. Obey today.

"Dear children, let us not love with words or tongue but with actions and in truth" (1 John 3:18). Loving God, help us to put our love into action.

I SHOW MY LOVE IN SERVICE TO OTHERS

THE PARABLE OF THE LONG LINE

The King's visit to Flibber-o-loo caused long lines of people pushing, shoving, and getting angry. They were so grouchy, they even pelted one another with Flibber berries!

But the Flibbians at the back of the line couldn't understand what all the fuss was about, so they stayed clear of the fighting.

When a cleaning man came out to serve everyone a cool drink, he observed the mess and began sweeping up the berries. But soon he found himself getting hit with Flibber berries too!

It was time for the King's appearance, and the cleaning man explained that he had the honor of choosing the first person to meet the King. He went to the end of the line and said, "Let's start here."

People were furious. "Hey! We're in front! What gives you the right to choose some- one from the back of the line?"

The cleaning man looked at them, smiled, and said, "Because I AM the King."

HE SERVANT KING

esus is King. But he is a servant King. When he came to earth, he served others—much like the King in Flibber-o-loo.

When we serve, we show God's love to others too. Some of Jesus' disciples had a hard time learning this lesson. Especially James and John.

WHAT DOES THE BIBLE SAY?

Matthew 20:20-24

One day, the mother of James and John Zebedee came to Jesus to ask a favor.

"Promise me that one of my two sons may sit at your right hand in your kingdom," Mrs. Zebedee said. "Promise that the other one may sit at your left hand."

You see, Mrs. Zebedee thought Jesus would be made a king very soon. She and her sons wanted Jesus to put them in the most important places next to the king.

When the other disciples found out about this, they were furious. They knew James and John and their mother were being selfish. It was like she was trying to let her sons cut to the front of the line.

Then Jesus said, "You know that some rulers like to act important and show their power. But my followers aren't like that. In my kingdom, if you want to be important, you must serve others like a servant."

Jesus explained that if you want to be first, you must be willing to be last—and put the needs of others in front of your own. Jesus was always willing to show his love for others by showing that he was willing to serve others. Are you?

BLE FACT:

ames and John were both fishermen when Jesus called them to be his disciples. When Jesus asked them to follow him, he asked them to be ishers of men!

BACKWARD DAY

Jesus said the first will be last and the last will be first. Celebrate this with "Backward Day." Try to do as many things backward as you can. Walk backwards around the house (but not on stairs). Eat dessert first. Hold your cereal spoon backwards. Wear your shirt inside out and backward.

Go into the week as a S.W.A.T. team member: **S**ervants **W**ith **A** **T**ray. Find ways to greet your family with service and a smile!

CUCUMBER CONNECTION

• Why do you think the King in the first story started at the end of the line?

• Jesus said that to be first, we must be last. What did he mean by that?

• What are the ways you serve others around the house? At school? Church? In your neighborhood?

THINK-LINK-ACT

THINK about the times you've pushed to be first. Will you give up your place and be last?

LINK that feeling to opportunities you have to put others first.

ACT on it by being a S.W.A.T. Team— **S**ervants **W**ith **A** **T**rash-Bag. Put your neighbors first by going through your neighborhood and picking up the trash.

"But I am among you as one who serves" (Luke 22:27b). Servant King, help us to love by serving one another.

PART FOUR

THE TRUST CONNECTION

CONNECTING TO TRUST WITH LIFE EXAMPLES FROM JOSEPH

The Trust Connection Verse

"May the God of hope fill you with
all joy and peace as you trust in him
so that you may overflow
with hope by the power of
the Holy Spirit."
(Romans 15:13)

WELCOME TO DODGEBALL CITY

YIPPEE KI-YAY KI-YAY! Today is a special day. YIPPEE KI-YAY KI-YOO! Today we welcome YOU!

Howdy, partners! Welcome to Dodgeball City, where our motto is: "Play fair or yer out!" My name is Bob the Tomato, and I'm the sheriff of this here town. It's an exciting place with desperados and heroes and tumbleweeds and dodge-balls, too, of course.

It's also the place where we're going to spend the next eight devotionals learning all about how to trust God.

In Dodgeball City, you're going to meet all sorts of fascinating folks. There's Mr. McPotipher. He owns the Rootin' Tootin' Pizza Place. We'll also meet twelve brothers who moseyed into town. They're cowboy peas with French accents: Reuben, Simeon, Levi, Izzy, Zeb, Gad, Ash, Dan, Natty, Jude, Baby Ben, and Little Joe.

Little Joe is the odd one of the bunch. He's a cucumber, not a pea. He also had some strange dreams—kind of like Joseph from the Bible. In fact, we're going to learn all about the real life of Joseph. But most of all, we're going to learn about trusting God even when things go wrong.

YIPPIE KI-YAY KI-YIM! It's time we trusted HIM!

GOD KNOWS WHAT'S BEST FOR ME

COWBOY SCHOOL

The first week of Cowboy School went great for Little Joe. He studied hard in Lasso class. He got an A in Moseying and a B in Playing Harmonica Around the Campfire.

His only problem was Bully the Kid.

One day during lunch, Little Joe was hopping back to his table and spotted Bully heading for his seat.

"Don't sit there!" Little Joe shouted.

"You gonna stop me?" snarled Bully.

"No . . . but trust me, you don't want to sit there," said Little Joe.

"You gonna give me trouble if I do? Ooooh, I'm shaking in my boots!"

"Trust me, you don't . . ."

Bully laughed and plopped down in Little Joe's seat. "YOWWWWWWWWW!" he yelled as he shot to the ceiling. He'd accidentally sat on Little Joe's science project—a cactus.

"I guess you didn't get my point," said Little Joe.

Actually, he got ten points—cactus points, that is—and they hurt something awful.

UPS AND DOWNS

Little Joe knew what was best for Bully the Kid. But the kid didn't trust him or listen. In the same way, God knows what's best for us. We just have to trust and listen.

In the Book of Genesis, a fellow named Joseph trusted God through some pretty tough times.

WHAT DOES THE BIBLE SAY?

Genesis 37:1–50:2b

Joseph's story starts off with a good old-fashioned feud—except it wasn't so good for Joseph. Because it's a really big story, here is a brief review of what's to come!

Joseph had ten older brothers and one younger brother. But his older brothers didn't like him. You'll find out next week the kind of mean things they did. But let's just say that Joseph ended up going through a lot of ups and downs.

DOWN: Joseph's brothers disliked him so much, they sold him.
DOWN: Joseph was made a slave.
UP: He became a really well-liked slave.
DOWN: He was blamed for a crime he didn't commit and thrown in jail.
UP: One of the king's helpers promised to talk the king into letting Joseph out of jail.
DOWN: The guy forgot all about Joseph and said nothing to the king.
UP: God was with Joseph and helped him interpret the king's dream.
UP: Joseph was made second in command in the entire country.
UP: Joseph forgave his brothers.

Through all of these ups and downs, Joseph trusted that God knew what was best for him. He knew God had big plans for his life, even though it was hard to see in the DOWN times.

Joseph also knew that with God, the UPs win out in the long run.

BIBLE FACT:

Joseph was sold to Midianite merchants in Egypt. Joseph was then sold to Potiphar, who was one of Pharaoh's officials. After being jailed by Potiphar, he became the second in command for the Pharaoh of Egypt.

CACTUS REMINDER

Buy a cactus and use it as a symbol of how God helps us through hard times. A cactus plant lives in a very tough place—the desert. But it survives because it can store a lot of water. The needles protect the cactus from animals that try to eat the plant for its water. God made the cactus to survive. Encourage everyone to participate in decorating the plant. Ask each family member to add his or her name; add the Connection Verse and anything else you would like.

Talk about the ways that God helps us to deal with tough times.

CUCUMBER CONNECTION

- Make a list of ups and downs you have gone through recently.

- How do you trust God when you're down?

- Read the Trust Connection Verse: Romans 15:13. How does trusting God give us hope?

THINK-LINK-ACT

THINK about something in which you need to listen and trust God with.

LINK it to a way in which God can help you by reading the Bible.

ACT on it and then journal ways in which reading the Bible and prayer have helped you to listen and trust God more.

"Those who know your name will trust in you, for you, LORD, have never forsaken those who seek you" (Psalm 9:10). God in heaven, we look to you always. We trust you.

Devotional - 26
AS GOOD AS GOLD

"We found gold!" shouted Little Joe. He dashed up to Mr. McPotipher with a pan overflowing with golden nuggets.

Little Joe and Mr. McPotipher had spent weeks panning for gold and dipping their pans in the stream, looking for pieces of gold in the water. They also battled coyotes, rattlesnakes, and dust storms.

A newspaper reporter was there to cover the excitement. "Does finding gold make you feel better about the problems you faced along the way?"

"No, laddie," said Mr. McPotipher. "GOD makes me feel better—not gold. When I've got problems, I trust in *him*."

Then Mr. McPotipher picked up a fork and took a bite of the "golden nuggets" in Little Joe's pan. "By the way, Little Joe, those are chicken nuggets—not gold. You grabbed the wrong pan."

"Oops."

Mr. McPotipher smiled at the reporter and said, "When I trust God, I can even survive a month with Little Joe!

HE DREAMER

Gold is one of the strongest things on earth. It can be battered and beaten and still stay in one piece. Even after a lot of wear and tear, it can be polished to sparkle and shine. If we trust God, we, too, can survive all kinds of difficulties and shine for God.

Joseph had his share of problems, but he stayed true to God. He had a heart of gold.

WHAT DOES THE BIBLE SAY?

Genesis 37:3-36

Joseph was a dreamer. But he had some strange dreams. He dreamed that his eleven brothers were stalks of wheat that bowed down to him. He also dreamed that his brothers were stars bowing down to him—as if they were his slaves!

Joseph told his brothers about the dreams, which probably wasn't the best idea. It made them furious. Even worse, they knew Joseph was the favorite son of their father, Jacob. Because Jacob loved Joseph so much, he gave him a beautiful coat of many colors.

One day, Jacob sent Joseph to check on his ten older brothers, who were watching sheep in the countryside. That's when the angry brothers hatched an evil plot.

They planned to kill Joseph.

The oldest son, Reuben, knew it was wrong. So he talked his brothers into throwing Joseph into a pit, secretly planning to go get him out once his brothers' tempers had calmed down. But his brothers decided it would be fitting to sell Joseph as a slave. After all, Joseph had dreamed that they were his slaves!

So Joseph went to Egypt as a slave, and his brothers let their father believe he had been killed by a wild animal.

Joseph was headed for some big-time problems, but he never lost faith. Joseph trusted God at all times.

BLE FACT:

The Robe of Many Colors—During Bible times robes were generally plain cloths used for warmth, trading, bundling things, and even for a loan guarantee. Joseph's robe, however, was ong, colorful, and richly decorated. This type of a robe was more often worn by royalty.

GOLD RUSH!

Have your own California Gold Rush. Find some large stones outside. Then spray-paint them gold and hide them in the house. Have the kids hunt for the gold. If they need help, tell them when they're "getting warmer" or "getting colder."

Write the words "Trust God" on the gold nuggets and keep them out on display as a reminder. Talk about how if we trust God, we have a heart of gold.

CUCUMBER CONNECTION

• How would you feel if your brothers did something mean to you?

• Why did Joseph trust God when bad things happened to him?

• Why do you trust (or not trust) the people around you? Why do you trust God?

THINK–LINK–ACT

THINK about a problem that you have right now.

LINK that problem to how you can trust God with it.

ACT on it through prayer. Then look for "gold" in the Bible. Hunt for verses that talk about how God can help in times of trouble.

"You are my fortress, my refuge in times of trouble" (Psalm 59:16b). Trustworthy Lord, help me to trust you with my problems so you can shine through me.

I WILL SHOW MY TRUST IN GOD BY OBEYING HIM

THE ROCKING HORSE RODEO

Yee-ha! All the greatest cowboys had gathered for the Rocking Horse Rodeo at the Okie Dokie Corral. Whoever stayed on the bustin' bronco rocking horse the longest would be the champ!

"Pssssst, Little Joe," whispered Bully the Kid. "If you wanna stay on your horse I've got some superglue."

"You wanna glue me to my saddle? That's CHEATING," said Little Joe.

"So what!" said Bully.

It was tempting, but Little Joe couldn't cheat. "No thanks."

Unfortunately, Little Joe's brother, Jude, gave in to the temptation and stayed on his rocking horse for a world record time!

"Hey Jude, you're champion!" announced the Mayor. "Come off your horse and get your trophy!"

Jude gulped. "Get off my horse? But . . . but . . . "

Jude COULDN'T get off his horse. In fact, he stayed glued to his horse for an entire month. Jude never got his trophy. He just got tired of sitting.

TRUE GRIT

Jude got himself into a pretty sticky situation. That usually happens when you give in to temptation.

In Egypt, Joseph had to fight temptation as well. But he found out that trusting God and doing what's right is better than doing what's wrong every time.

WHAT DOES THE BIBLE SAY?

Genesis 39:1-20a

Joseph became a slave for an important palace captain in Egypt. This captain, named Potiphar, really liked Joseph. So he let Joseph work inside his beautiful house.

One day, Potiphar's wife tried to trick Joseph into coming with her, which was very wrong, because she was married. She was very pretty, so it was tempting! But Joseph said, "No! I choose to obey God."

Potiphar's wife got really mad, and she tried to tempt him again the next day. And the next day. And the next!

"No!" Joseph said. "Your husband trusts me! I will obey God! You should too."

Joseph had true grit, which means he was determined to do what was right and stay honest.

Finally, Potiphar's wife got so angry that she decided to do something really mean. She told her husband, Potiphar, a lie. She said that Joseph had harmed her.

Potiphar believed his wife's lies and threw Joseph into jail. But even in jail, Joseph continued to trust that God still had a plan for his life.

BIBLE FACT:

Trusted Slave—It wasn't unusual for a foreign slave like Joseph to be given an important job—if he was trustworthy.

JCKING BRONCO RELAY

Hold a Bucking Bronco relay: bounce eally small children up and down on our knees, let children enjoy a ride on our back, or tell everyone to get down in all fours and pretend to be a bucking bronco. (Add a stuffed animal on each other's backs for more fun!) Race from one area of the room (or yard) to the other!

When the race is over, talk about how staying on a bucking bronco is a lot like everyday life—sometimes it's hard to stay on the right path! How can you help each other as family to obey God every day?

CUCUMBER CONNECTION

- What is temptation?
- What temptations do you face?
- How do you battle your temptations?

THINK-LINK-ACT

THINK about something wrong that can be tempting to you.

LINK that temptation to how trusting in God can help you to fight temptation and continue to obey God.

ACT on it by writing down how you can trust God with your temptation. Put it in a safe place. Pray for God's help. Take it out and read it each week and see if you're getting better at doing what's right.

God is faithful; he will not let you be tempted beyond what you can bear" 1 Corinthians 10:13b). Loving God, when I'm tempted to do something wrong, help me learn that I can always trust you.

Devotional - 28

THE GOOD, THE BAD, AND THE SILLY

Sheriff Bob stopped a ketchup fight at the Rootin' Tootin' Pizza Place. Then he captured "shopping cart" rustlers at the local grocery store.

"How do you keep such a good attitude?" asked Little Joe.

"I trust God," said Bob. "I'm joyful knowing that God is watching over me every minute of the day."

"Wow!" Little Joe smiled.

"Of course, God makes my job easier than you might think."

"How's that?"

Sheriff Bob nodded toward three crooks robbing the Dodgeball City Bank.

"How are we supposed to wear these bandanas?" one of them asked as he tied it over his eyes.

Another crook was wearing his like a babushka, while the third one was trying to look like a cowboy.

"Follow me, boys," said Sheriff Bob as he tied their bandanas together like a rope, lassoed the crooks, and led them off to jail.

"I see what you mean," laughed Little Joe.

HE PRISONER

heriff Bob had a good attitude. He wasn't an ornery cowpoke. No fussin' or omplainin' from him. He trusted God. He even trusted that God was making his job asier for him!

oseph had a great attitude too, even in a tough place like prison. This led to some mazing things that happened!

WHAT DOES THE BIBLE SAY?

Genesis 39:20b-23

Prison was no picnic. It was tough on Joseph. But amazingly enough, oseph never stopped trusting God.

Prison was also a tough job for the warden—the guy in charge of the ail. He had a lot of responsibility! He had to keep all of the prisoners ocked up. He made sure they were ed. He helped the prisoners when hey got sick. And he stopped ights.

Back in those days, the warden could use prisoners to help him with all of this work. But the prisoners had to be trustworthy.

The warden saw right away that Joseph was different. Joseph's good attitude showed up as soon as he got there. It was also clear that Joseph loved and obeyed God. He didn't get into fights, and he helped others without being asked.

So the warden put Joseph in charge of all the prisoners!

Once again, Joseph found himself in a tough spot where good things began to happen. Joseph didn't know what would happen next! But good or bad, Joseph was ready to trust God.

BIBLE FACT:

The king's prisoner — Joseph was considered a "king's prisoner." King's prisoners were treated better than other prisoners.

DON'T LOOK NOW!

Ask everyone in the family to draw a cowboy-related picture—a horse, sheriff, cactus, and so on. Then color it in. But there's a catch! You all have to do it BLINDFOLDED. Be sure to help one another by coaching each other along!

Talk about how our problems can be as hard as drawing blindfolded. That's why we need God by our side to coach us along.

CUCUMBER CONNECTION

- Life isn't always fair. What unfair things have happened to you?

- What was your attitude like in those situations? Did you trust God?

- How does trusting God help us have a good attitude?

THINK-LINK-ACT

THINK about a time that you felt very alone.

LINK that feeling to what would have happened if you had remembered that God was right by your side!

ACT on it by trusting that God is always with you, every day, no matter where you go!

"In God I trust. I will not be afraid. What can mortal man do to me?" (Psalm 56:4b). God, help me to be joyful even when things aren't fair.

I WILL TRUST GOD TO GIVE ME COURAGE

HIGH NOON

Sheriff Bob looked at his digital watch. It read, "High Noon."

It was time for his showdown with Bully the Kid, the biggest bully in Dodgeball City.

Even though the sheriff was scared, he knew someone had to stand up to that bully. He trusted God to help him be brave.

"I didn't think ya had the guts," growled Bully as they stood back to back in the dusty street. "Count off four steps. Then turn and throw your dodgeball!"

As Bob and Bully counted out the steps, they hopped away from each other.

"1 . . . 2 . . . 3 . . . !"

At the count of four, Bob whirled around. But Bully the Kid kept hopping and counting, "22 . . . 45 . . . 7 . . . 67 . . . 19 . . . !" Bully didn't know how to count. So he just kept counting and hopping away. In fact, he hopped right out of town. Maybe he's still hopping today!

"That's one way to get a bully out of town," said Bob with a smile.

99

JAIL BIRDS

Having courage means being brave. That doesn't mean you never feel scared. It means doing what's right, even when you're scared silly. Sheriff Bob knew that, and so did Joseph. Joseph had to trust God for courage while he was in the Egyptian prison.

WHAT DOES THE BIBLE SAY?

Genesis 40:1-23

Joseph wasn't the only one who had been hurled into jail. So had the king's baker and cupbearer.

One night, the baker and cupbearer both had strange dreams. Because God had given Joseph the ability to understand what dreams meant, they both told Joseph about their dreams.

Joseph told the cupbearer that his dream was good news! The cupbearer had dreamed about three grapevines that blossomed and grew grapes that made juice for Pharaoh. That meant that in three days he would get out of jail and get his job back!

Joseph told the baker that his dream was bad news. The baker had

dreamed that birds were eating out of the three baskets of bread. Joseph was sad about what he had to tell the baker, but God gave him courage. Joseph told the baker that in three days Pharaoh was going to have him killed.

Sure enough, both of Joseph's predictions were true.

After being freed, the cupbearer promised to talk to the king about getting Joseph out of jail. But he soon forgot, and Joseph stayed in prison for a long time.

Joseph was disappointed, but trusted God and faced his future with courage.

BIBLE FACT:

The Cupbearer—In Bible times, a cupbearer had a pretty dangerous job. His job was to taste the king's food and drink it to make sure it wasn't poisoned. Talk about bravery!

HO'S AFRAID?

sk each family member to write down omething he or she is afraid of onto a iece of paper. Tape each paper onto a eparate two-liter soda bottle and fill alf of it with water. Set up the bottles

in the backyard. Take turns trying to knock them down with a dodgeball.

When the game is over, talk about how God gives us courage to help us defeat our fears.

CUCUMBER CONNECTION

• Joseph had to be brave when he told the baker about what would happen to him. He also had to face his future with courage.

• When does it take bravery for you to tell the truth?

• How does God give you courage?

THINK-LINK-ACT

THINK about something that requires you to be brave.

LINK that to different ways that God gives us courage.

ACT on it by talking to God about your fear and trusting him to be brave!

Do not be terrified; do not be discouraged, for the LORD your God will be with you wherever you go" (Joshua 1:9b). Precious God, thank you for being with me, even when I'm afraid.

Devotional - 30

THE COWBOY WHO CRIED "STAMPEDE!"

"STAMPEDE!" Little Joe shouted, dashing into camp.

The French Pea cowboys knew what would happen if they got caught in the path of charging buffalo.

"E-gad! Save yourself!" Reuben yelled to his brother, who was trying to save their lunch.

"Forget Reuben's sandwich!" shouted Gad.

"Hey Jude! Give me a boost into that tree," Levi called.

Soon, Little Joe and the cowboy peas were all safe in the trees. They prayed for God's protection from the stampede.

Then an enormous herd of gophers scurried through camp!

"Uh . . . Little Joe . . . was THAT the stampede?"

"Yup," said Little Joe. "It was a gopher stampede. I didn't say it was buffalo, did I?"

The peas watched in shock as the gophers ran off with their lunch . . . and Levi's jeans.

"LITTLE JOE! You better head for the hills!"

Suddenly, Little Joe had another reason to pray.

HE KING'S DREAM

ome people only pray to God when they think they're in trouble—like during a tampede. But to be friends with God, we need to talk to him every day. We should pray in good times and in bad times. That's how we can get to know God better, which will build our trust in him.

oseph had this kind of relationship with God. Maybe that's why God spoke to him n so many ways—including dreams.

WHAT DOES THE BIBLE SAY?

Genesis 41:1-45

oseph was stuck in prison for many years. But that all changed when the king of Egypt suddenly ordered Joseph out of jail so that he could explain the king's dreams.

The king dreamed he saw seven fat cows come out of the Nile River to eat grass. Then seven ugly, skinny cows came out of the river and swallowed up the seven fat cows. In another dream, he saw seven tall, strong plants. Then seven shriveled plants grew up and ate the strong plants.

"I can explain your dreams with God's help," Joseph told the king.

So Joseph explained that the king's dreams meant there would be seven years of good crops followed by seven terrible years without food. Joseph told the king to store up food during the good years so that people wouldn't starve during the bad years.

The king was so amazed that he put Joseph in charge of the plan. In the blink of an eye, Joseph became the second most powerful man in Egypt, under the king. Joseph's relationship with God had served him well. God had richly blessed Joseph after he had showed his loyal trust in God.

IBLE FACT:

Lord of the Ring—The Pharaoh let Joseph use his signet ring. The ring showed that Joseph had been given great power.

FRIENDSHIP CHAIN

Cut out strips of construction paper to create a paper chain. Write a characteristic of friendship onto each strip of paper. Loop the strips together and tape the links in place. Every day, tear off one link and talk about how you can develop that friendship characteristic with God. Then pray about it.

Pharaoh gave Joseph a ring to show him that he was important to his kingdom. We are important to God's kingdom too! That's why God wants a personal relationship with each one of us.

CUCUMBER CONNECTION

- How do you get to be friends with someone?
- What's the best part about friendship?
- How do your friendships compare with your God relationship?

THINK-LINK-ACT

THINK about ways you need to make your friendship better with God.

LINK that to the qualities you look for in a friendship. Apply them to your relationship with God.

ACT on it by setting aside a time each day to pray and read from the Bible. This will make your relationship with God stronger.

"I will make you like my signet ring for I have chosen you, declares the LORD Almighty" (Haggai 2:23b). Loving Father, I want you to be my best friend! Help me to get to know you better every day of my life!

I WILL TRUST GOD'S PLAN

THE PIZZA COWBOY

The Pony Express Pizza Delivery was the fastest in the land. One day, Little Joe rode two hundred miles to deliver a pizza just to find out that the order was a bad joke. No one had really ordered it!

"Well . . . at least I helped a guy pull his stagecoach out of the mud on the way here!" he said. What Little Joe didn't know was:

- By getting the stagecoach out of the mud, the sheriff was able to get to Dodgeball City just in time to stop a bank robbery.

- By stopping the robbery, the town could afford to build a new hospital.

- The hospital saved the lives of many people, including a famous preacher.

- The preacher led hundreds of people to God, including Little Joe's nephews.

So God took something bad and turned it into something good!

If only Little Joe knew . . .

"Mmmmmmm, cheesy crust," muttered Little Joe. Then he took a big bite of pizza and rode off into the sunset.

SAVING EGYPT

When Little Joe was tricked into delivering a pizza, God turned it into something good. But he didn't know that would happen at the time.

When Joseph's brothers sold him as a slave, God also turned it into something good. But he didn't know that would happen at the time.

But God knew. That's why we must trust in God's plan, not our own.

WHAT DOES THE BIBLE SAY?

Genesis 41:41-45:15

Pharaoh's dream came true. Just as Joseph said, Egypt had seven straight years of wonderful crops. They had more food than they could eat.

So Joseph made sure the Egyptians saved up food for the coming bad years. He had Egyptians in every city build huge silos. (Silos are tall, round buildings for storing food.)

The second part of the king's dream also came true. The ground dried up, and the land suffered during the seven terrible years. No food grew in the fields. But because

Joseph trusted God's plan, there wa plenty of food stored up in Egypt.

However, this famine hit more than Egypt. It struck the land of Canaan where Joseph had grown up. Back home, Joseph's family was starving. But Joseph's father, Jacob, heard there was food stored in silos in Egypt. So he sent his ten older sons to Egypt to bring food back.

Jacob had no idea that he was sending his sons straight into the arms of his long-lost son, Joseph. He had no idea what was going to happen. But God did!

BIBLE FACT:

A New Name—The Pharaoh gave Joseph a new Egyptian name—Zaphenath-Paneah.

PIZZA PLANS

Make a homemade pizza as a family. Talk about how a recipe is a plan. As you enjoy the pizza, make some other plans for things you can do as a family.

Talk about ways in which your plans could change. Are there some things that God may have a hand in changing? What will you do if your plans do change? How will you show your trust in God if plans change?

CUCUMBER CONNECTION

- How do you feel when something bad happens?

- When we trust God's plan, how does that help us to deal with bad things that happen?

- What can you do to help you wait to find out what God's plan is during tough times?

THINK-LINK-ACT

THINK about a plan that you had that didn't go as you had expected.

LINK that to what you have learned about trusting God's plan. What can you do the next time that happens?

ACT on it by praying to God every day. God loves you and has a plan for every day of your life. Trust him with it!

"Trust in the LORD and do good; dwell in the land and enjoy safe pasture" (Psalm 37:3). Awesome God, your way is the best way. Help me to trust your plans.

I WILL SHOW MY TRUST IN GOD TO OTHERS

Devotional - 32

THE FORGIVING COWBOY

On the last day of Cowboy School, Little Joe decided to trust God with the hardest thing he had ever done—he told Bully the Kid that he forgave him for being mean.

"Thanks, partner," said Bully. "No one's ever been nice to me before. Can you help me change?"

"God can help you change, and I'll be there rootin' you on, partner!"

So Bully and Little Joe became friends. Since they were official "cowpokes," they decided they would poke some cows before they left.

Bully and Joe didn't realize that "cowpoke" is just another word for cowboy. It doesn't mean you're supposed to poke cows. But that wasn't their only problem . . .

"Uh . . . Bully . . . I don't think we just poked a cow!"

"What do you mean?"

"IT WAS A BULL!"

The two cowpokes ran for their lives. Cowboy School was over, but they still had a lot to learn.

G PLANS

Little Joe showed others how he trusted God by forgiving Bully the Kid.

Joseph also had a chance to show forgiveness to his brothers—in a most amazing way.

WHAT DOES THE BIBLE SAY?

Genesis 42:1–50:21

Remember a long time ago when Joseph dreamed that his brothers would bow down to him? Well . . . it happened!

When Joseph's ten older brothers came to Egypt, they didn't recognize their brother. They bowed down to him and begged for food.

Joseph wanted to find out if his brothers had changed after what they had done to him. So he accused their youngest brother, Benjamin, of stealing a very expensive gold cup (even though it wasn't true). Then he threw Benjamin in jail.

Joseph's brothers were so upset that they asked to be put in prison in Benjamin's place. They were willing to

go to prison for their little brother. That's when Joseph knew they had truly changed.

So Joseph told his brothers who he was. He also told them that he forgave them. His brothers had wronged him by selling him as a slave and lying to their father by letting him believe that he had been killed. But God had turned it into something good. Joseph was able to save both Egypt and his family from starving.

God had big plans for Joseph. God has big plans for you too! That's why you have to trust him with everything that happens. After all, God made you special—and he loves you very much!

BLE FACT:

Twelve Tribes—Jacob's twelve sons went on to lead twelve different family groups called the tribes of Israel. Jesus was descended from the tribe of Judah.

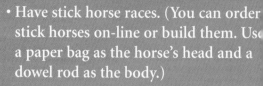

Family Fun Connection:

COWBOY PICNIC

End your time in Dodgeball City with a cowboy picnic:

- Dress up as cowboys and cowgirls.
- Play dodgeball with soft foam balls.
- Eat beans and franks.

- Have stick horse races. (You can order stick horses on-line or build them. Use a paper bag as the horse's head and a dowel rod as the body.)
- Set up a pretend campfire. Put a flashlight under some sticks or rocks. Sing songs. Eat marshmallows. Tell Bible stories about people who trusted God. Talk about how you will trust in God's plan in the future.

CUCUMBER CONNECTION

- Look at the timeline of Joseph's story. What are all the different ways that Joseph trusted God?

- Look at your own timeline. In what ways ha you trusted God?

- How can you trust God more in the future?

THINK-LINK-ACT

THINK about someone you know who has trouble trusting God.

LINK that person to God by praying that God will help you to find a way to reach them with his message.

ACT on it by inviting that person to church. Give him or her a Bible. Think of other ways to reach that person with God's love.

"Commit your way to the LORD; trust in him and he will do this: He will make your righteousness shine like the dawn, the justice of your cause like the noonday sun" (Psalm 37:5–6). Lord, help us to show how much we trust you by shining with your love.

PART FIVE

THE TiME CONNECTiON

CONNECTING TO TIME THROUGH THE WRITINGS OF THE DISCIPLE JOHN

The Time Connection Verse

"Teach us to number our days aright,
that we may gain a heart of wisdom."
(Psalm 90:12)

"Teach us to make the most of our time,
so that we may grow in wisdom."
(Psalm 90:12 NLT)

WELCOME TO THE CHOCOLATE FACTORY

Good morning, folks. How are you? I hope you're feeling fine. I'd love to stay and talk, but it's almost eight o'clock. And I haven't got the time.

My name is Laura Carrot, and I deliver milk to the Nezzer Chocolate Factory every morning at precisely eight o'clock. If I'm even a minute late, Mr. Nezzer takes away some of my pay.

Time is very important at the chocolate factory. As Mr. Nezzer always says, "Time is money." In fact, time is what we're going to be learning about in this section of the family devotional, because time is very, very important to God. But not for the same reasons that it's important to Mr. Nezzer— he still has a lot to learn about that!

Time is very important to God because he wants to spend time with us. That means we have to make time for him. It also means we have to think about how we spend our time, and make sure that we use it wisely. God also wants us to use our time in good ways like loving and serving others.

So hop into my flying milk truck, and I'll take you to the chocolate factory. You'll get to meet all kinds of people, like Rack, Shack, and Benny—a tomato, asparagus, and cucumber that work for Mr. Nezzer. They are really good about spending a lot of their time the way God would want them to. You'll also get to meet Mr. Nezzer and his assistant, Mr. Lunt.

If you're good, maybe I'll even give you a chocolate bunny.

GOD IS ETERNAL

HE BUNNY!

Mr. Nezzer had created a giant chocolate bunny and placed it right outside his chocolate factory.

"Everyone shall *eternally* bow down to this bunny!" Mr. Nezzer shouted.

"What does *eternal* mean, boss?" asked Mr. Lunt, his assistant.

"It means the bunny will last FOREVER. So everyone bow down and sing the Bunny Song!"

The bunny, the bunny. How I love the bunny!
I didn't eat my soup or my bread—just the bunny.
The bunny, the bunny. Oh! I love the bunny!
That's all I want to buy with any of my money!

"Excuse me, boss," said Mr. Lunt. "Look at the bunny."

Mr. Nezzer looked up and saw that the giant bunny had melted into a sticky puddle of chocolate in the hot sun.

Mr. Lunt pulled out his pocket watch. "Is fifteen minutes eternal, boss?"

Mr. Nezzer just growled. Fifteen minutes was *not* eternal.

FOREVER ETERNAL

The bunny was anything but eternal. After all, eternal *means* forever. And the bunny couldn't even last fifteen minutes!

God, however, *is* eternal. He is forever with us. The apostle John made this very clear in his writings in the Bible.

WHAT DOES THE BIBLE SAY?

John 1:1-18, 1 John 5:13-18

Think back in time. Think back farther than your great-great-great-great-great-grandparents.

In fact, think farther back than the Romans. Farther back than Adam and Eve. Keep going! Think back before the creation of the sun and the moon. Back to the beginning of time!

What do we know about the beginning of time, when the world didn't even exist? We don't have many answers, but we do know this: there was God!

In the beginning, there was God, says John the disciple. That's because God is eternal. That means that God is forever!

But that's not all. John says that Jesus was God, and through Jesus, God stepped down into our time. He lived on earth as a human.

When Jesus died, he was buried. But he rose three days later! That's because Jesus will live forever!

But there's even more good news! Jesus lives forever, and if we follow him, we will live forever too! We will have eternal life and live forever with God. That's the wonderful gift that our eternal God offers to all of us!

BIBLE FACT:

The Word—Jesus was there at the beginning of time. The Gospel of John says that the Word was with God in the beginning. The "Word" is a special name for Jesus.

TOP TIME / START TIME

Play "Stop Time / Start Time" just like the old game: "Red Light / Green Light."

The person who is "it" stands with his back to everyone. When he says, "Start Time," people move toward him across the room or the yard. When he says, "Stop Time," he whirls around as everyone freezes. If he sees someone moving, they go back to the beginning. The others stay frozen until he turns his back and says, "Start Time" again.

Keep playing until someone crosses the finish line and tags the person who is "it" without being seen moving.

CUCUMBER CONNECTION

• Jesus promises us eternal life in heaven. What do you think heaven will be like?

• If you could go back in time and meet someone from the Bible, who would it be?

• How can you help tell others about the gift of eternal life?

THINK-LINK-ACT

THINK about how it feels when someone dies.

LINK those feelings to how you follow Jesus.

ACT on it by remembering God's promise of eternal life if you follow Jesus! Remember that life in heaven never ends when you love and follow Jesus!

"The eternal God is your refuge, and underneath are the everlasting arms" (Deuteronomy 33:27). Lord, thank you for saving us so that we can have eternal life and live forever in heaven with you!

Devotional - 34

LIFE IS LIKE A BOX OF CHOCOLATES

Laura Carrot took her good friend, Forest Grape, on a tour through the Chocolate Factory.

"Life is like a box of chocolates," Forest Grape said, munching on a chocolate bunny. "You never know what you're gonna get!"

As Laura showed him around, Forest walked under a spilling vat of hot chocolate! But Laura yanked him to safety, just in the nick of time! Then Forest caught his shirt in the conveyor belt. But Laura saved him just in the nick of time! When Forest chased a feather right into the box-wrapping machine, Laura saved him, just in the nick of time!

After the tour, Laura and Forest sat together and ate another chocolate bunny.

"Hey, Laura. You've got chocolate on your mouth," Forest told her.

"Thanks, Forest!"

"I thought I'd save you from getting embarrassed! Maybe someday you can save me too."

"I'll sure try," said Laura with a big grin.

EST FRIENDS

t's true. You never know what's going to happen next in life. That's why it's good to
ave family and friends to help you out. That's also why God sent us the greatest
Friend we could ever ask for.

WHAT DOES THE BIBLE SAY?

John 14:15-29

id you know you've got an invisible Friend who's with you every second of every minute of every hour of every day?

No, this is not an imaginary friend. It is the Holy Spirit.

When Jesus was having his last meal on earth, he told his disciples he was going to send them a Friend. And this Friend would be with them all of the time. He was talking about the Holy Spirit.

There is one God, but he can be seen in three different ways. There is God the Father, God the Son

(Jesus), and God the Holy Spirit.

Jesus explained that the Holy Spirit would live inside us. The Holy Spirit is always there to help us— just like Laura was there to help her friend Forest in the Chocolate Factory.

Jesus told us that the Holy Spirit loves us. The Holy Spirit teaches us the difference between right and wrong. He helps us to understand the Bible. He encourages us. And he helps us know what to do when the unexpected happens.

That's what Friends are for!

IBLE FACT:

Pentecost—The Holy Spirit came to more than three thousand people during the festival of Pentecost in Acts 2.

POWER SOURCE

Secretly unplug your CD player. When you gather for family fun, attempt to play some music on it. Then wonder why it isn't working and ask the kids to help you figure out why. After you figure it out, explain that just like the CD player gets power from being connected to electricity, we also get power from the Holy Spirit to connect to God.

Unlike electricity, however, the Holy Spirit is with us all the time! That's because when we put our trust in God, the Holy Spirit become a constant power source in our life. Play som music as you pass around a "hot potato." When the music stops, the person with the h potato should talk about a situation in which it's helpful to know that the Holy Spirit is wi you all the time!

CUCUMBER CONNECTION

- Who is the Holy Spirit?
- How can the Holy Spirit help you?
- How is the Holy Spirit different from God the Father and God the Son?

THINK-LINK-ACT

THINK about a problem in which it's nice to have someone to help you decide between right and wrong.

LINK that decision to having the Holy Spirit as a constant connection to God with you all the time!

ACT on it by listening to the Holy Spirit so that you can make the right choice! Pray for the Holy Spirit to guide you every day.

"Dear friends, build yourselves up in your most holy faith and pray in the Holy Spirit" (Jude 1:20). Lord, thank you for sending a Friend who can be with us all the time.

I WILL SPEND TIME WITH GOD

LIGHTS OUT!

As the lights went out in the Chocolate Factory,

Bob shouted, "Blackout!"

"Keep working!" yelled Mr. Lunt. "We have 14,638 chocolate bunnies to make today."

"I can't see! What's this?"

"That's my nose! OOF!"

"Keep working!"

After fifteen minutes of bumbling around in the dark, the lights came back on. Amazing— they had created the largest piece of chocolate ever!

"Not bad for working in the dark," Mr. Lunt observed.

"Not bad? It's terrible!" said Bob, who was covered in chocolate.

Mr. Lunt turned to Larry. "No more working in the dark."

"Gee Bob, you're such a sweet guy now!" Larry said.

Bob just groaned.

THE POWER OF LIGHT

You can't make chocolate in the dark without making a major mess. In the same way, you can't walk through life without God's light. Without it, you'll always end up in a big mess!

WHAT DOES THE BIBLE SAY?

1 John 1:5–2:6

A re you afraid of the dark? Some people are.

But some people actually like the dark because they think they can hide the bad things they do. Robbers like to work at night so they can sneak around and not be seen.

In the Bible, John wrote that some people "walk in darkness." He is using the word "darkness" to describe sin, which is disobeying God.

John said we all sin. If you think you don't sin, you're just fooling yourself. We sin by many things that we do—and by many things that we don't do. But don't worry!

When we let God's light into our life, that light can help us to over-power sin.

Think about it. Light is stronger than dark. Whenever light shines into a room, darkness goes away. It's not the other way around. You can't shine beams of darkness into a light room. Flashlights cut through the darkness. But there are no such things as "Flashdarks." Darkness is not stronger than light.

So walk in God's light. Read your Bible. Pray. Spend time with God.

We never have to fear the dark because when we walk with God, we are also walking in the light!

BIBLE FACT:

The Beloved—John was sometimes called "the beloved disciple" because he was so close to Jesus. He walked in God's light.

ASHLIGHT TAG

lay flashlight tag in the house with the
ghts out. Everyone hides. Then the
erson who is "it" hunts for everyone
lse with a flashlight. If he "tags" some-

one with the flashlight, they're out.
Keep going until everyone is found.
The last person found is the winner.

*Be sure that really little ones are paired with
Mom or Dad for this activity!*

CUCUMBER CONNECTION

- Why does John use "darkness" to describe sin?

- What is sin?

- How does God's light help you to fight sin?

THINK-LINK-ACT

THINK about something that you have done wrong.

LINK God's light to what you did wrong. If you shine God's light on it, was it easy to see the wrong you did?

ACT on it as a family by shining God's light into your life every day. Tell God and others in your family one thing you've done wrong and ask them to forgive you.

Jesus] said, 'I am the light of the world. Whoever follows me will never walk in dark-
ess, but will have the light of life'" (John 8:12). Light of the world, shine your light
nto our lives every moment of the day!

Devotional - 36

BREAKDOWN!

Mr. Nezzer didn't believe in fixing the machinery in the Chocolate Factory. So as you might guess, it broke down.

"Get it fixed NOW!" Mr. Nezzer yelled.

"But boss, you fired the repairman—to save money," said Mr. Lunt.

"Then YOU fix it!"

Mr. Lunt saw that the pipes carrying chocolate had come apart. But there were so many pipes, he didn't know which ones to connect together. So he took a guess.

He accidentally connected the cold water pipe to the milk pipe. He sent sugar where the drinking water was supposed to go. And where did the chocolate go?

Let's check in with Bob the Tomato. As you recall, Bob got covered with chocolate during the blackout.

"It'll be nice to wash all of this chocolate off of me," said Bob as he stepped into the shower. Singing a happy song, Bob turned on the shower and . . .

"AAAAHHHHHH!"

He discovered where the chocolate was now flowing.

HE VINE

Mr. Nezzer didn't think making repairs was important. The result was a disaster. Chocolate came out of the shower pipes and onto Bob!

In the Bible, John warns us what can happen if we don't make God important in our lives. Here's a hint: it's a lot worse than a chocolaty shower.

WHAT DOES THE BIBLE SAY?

John 15:1-17

Jesus said that he is the vine and we are the branches. If we don't stay connected to the vine, we've got big problems. Just like the branches and leaves of a plant have to stay connected to the vine or the trunk in order to live, Jesus is also saying that we must stay connected to him. If we do, our lives will be filled with love, joy, peace, patience, kindness, goodness, faithfulness, gentleness, and self-control. If we don't stay connected, we cannot receive these wonderful gifts.

To keep a vine alive, we must water it and give it air. We also have to prune or cut away the bad branches. In order to stay connected to Jesus, we have to prioritize our time and make godly choices. We can do this by praying, reading the Bible, showing love to others, going to church, and obey God's teachings.

We also need to connect with God in these ways on a regular basis every day, not just when things go wrong. That would be like repairing factory machinery only when things break down. God needs to be our priority—the most important thing in our life.

If we stay connected to Jesus, we will continue to grow strong and beautiful, and we will show others that we are connected to Jesus by our actions.

BLE FACT:

Fruit of the Spirit—The Bible lists the fruit of the Spirit—love, joy, peace, patience, kindness, goodness, faithfulness, gentleness, and self-control (Galatians 5:22—23).

"TOP TEN" LISTS

Ask every family member to name the top ten things that are important to them. Write each of them down on a separate sheet of paper. If you have enough separate rooms in the house, allow each person to hide his or her priorities in a different room. If you don't have enough rooms, then take turns hiding the clues in one or two rooms. Be sure that all clues are visible in some way! (Otherwise it will be too hard.)

Assign each person someone else's priorities. Then race against time to try and find them. Once they are found, the finder should try to guess the correct order. Finish by asking each person to reveal the correct order. Discuss the outcome and how you can all work harder to place godly priorities first!

CUCUMBER CONNECTION

- How is Jesus like the vine, and how are we like the branches?

- What happens if you don't stay connected to Jesus?

- How can you make God important in your life?

THINK-LINK-ACT

THINK about the ways in which you let other things take priority over God.

LINK those things to a list of things that you have to do in the following week.

ACT: On it by figuring out how to place God first in the days ahead.

"[Bear] fruit in every good work, growing in the knowledge of God" (Colossians 1:10b). Jesus, help us to connect with you every day. Help us grow strong.

I WILL TRUST GOD'S TIMING

CHOCOLATE MONSTERS

Everything was timed just right at the Nezzer Chocolate Factory.

Machines came together to make each part of the chocolate bunny. A mechanical hand placed the ears on each bunny's head, as two brushes painted black button eyes, and a series of twirling arms slapped yellow bowties in place.

"Make it go faster!" yelled Bubba Pea, an impatient employee. When no one was looking, he turned the dial to "Super Fast."

MASH! BAM! SPLURT! SMOOSH!

Everything went faster and faster. The machines smashed together, and the chocolate flew! The cute little bunnies soon looked like chocolate monsters. The wildly moving hands gave each bunny strange-looking ears. The brushes slopped giant eyes on each one.

"Faster! Faster!" Bubba yelled. But Mr. Nezzer shut it down just before the machinery exploded.

When Mr. Nezzer opened the boxes, inside was a chocolate mess.

"We could call them Chocolate Mutants, boss," suggested Mr. Lunt.

Mr. Nezzer growled.

"Or not," added Mr. Lunt.

DEAD MAN WALKING

The machinery in a chocolate factory is timed just right. Everything has to be done at the exact moment of time. If the timing is off, there's a big mess.

God does things in his own special timing too. Unfortunately, we're a lot like Bubba—we don't like to wait! When things don't happen fast enough for us, we become impatient, confused, or even angry. Two friends of Jesus didn't understand that he wants us to trust in God's timing. Their names are Mary and Martha.

WHAT DOES THE BIBLE SAY?

John 11:1-44

Lazarus was dying. His two sisters, Mary and Martha, were good friends of Jesus. So when Lazarus became sick, they sent a message to Jesus begging him to come quickly.

Jesus loved Lazarus, Mary, and Martha very much. But Jesus didn't come right away, and while they waited, Lazarus died.

Mary and Martha were very sad and confused. Why didn't Jesus come in time to heal Lazarus?

Finally, four days after Lazarus died, Jesus came to their town. Martha ran to Jesus, saying that if he had come sooner, her brother would not have died.

Jesus answered, "Your brother will rise again." Then he told the people to open Lazarus's tomb.

"But Lord," said Martha. "By this time there is a bad smell. Lazarus has been in the tomb for four days."

That didn't stop Jesus. He called out to Lazarus by name, and the dead man came out. He was still wrapped up with grave clothes around his face and body—like a mummy.

It was all about God's timing, and it was time for Lazarus to live again.

BIBLE FACT:

Jesus Wept—The shortest verse in the Bible is John 11:35: "Jesus wept." Why do you think Jesus cried? Because of the death of his friend, Lazarus? Because Mary and Martha didn't trust him to take care of Lazarus? Or because Jesus knew that all of us have trouble trusting in God's timing?

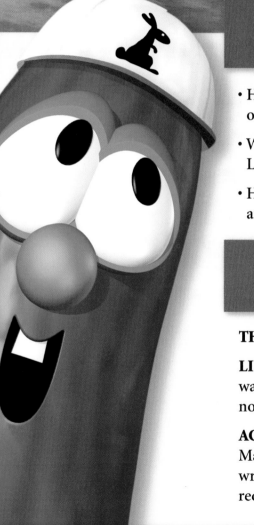

ZARUS LIVES

ct out the story of Lazarus. A parent
nould read the story right from the
ible, while the others act out the other
bles. For simple costumes, kids can
wear robes and towels for their head
coverings. Wrap "Lazarus" in toilet
tissue. If you have a video camera, film
the story.

CUCUMBER CONNECTION

- How would you have felt if you were Mary or Martha?

- Why do you think Jesus waited to help Lazarus?

- How do you think Mary and Martha felt after Lazarus came out of the tomb?

THINK-LINK-ACT

THINK about things that make you impatient.

LINK those things to reasons why we must wait for things to happen in God's timing, not our own.

ACT on it by finding ways to be patient. Make a prayer calendar. Use black ink to write down things you are waiting for. Use red ink to write down answers to prayers.

or the LORD is a God of justice. Blessed are all who wait for him"
saiah 30:18b). Lord, help me to wait for blessings from you.

I WILL MAKE GOOD USE OF MY TIME

THE NOSE KNOWS

There was big trouble at the Chocolate Factory. The steel tank containing chocolate started to crack.

"Plug the hole with your finger!" Larry shouted.

"We don't have fingers," Bob noted.

"I'll use my nose!" Junior Asparagus offered.

When another crack formed, Larry stuck his nose in the hole. When another crack formed, Bob stuck his nose in the hole. Pretty soon, eight workers stood around with Junior, plugging holes with their noses.

That's when Mr. Nezzer wandered by. "Why are all of you just standing there?" he shouted. "That's not good use of your time!"

"But . . ."

"I don't pay you to stand around!"

"But . . ."

"Get back to work . . . NOW!"

The eight workers shrugged and pulled their noses out of the holes. SPLAAAAT!! Chocolate shot out from the holes and smacked Mr. Nezzer clear into the next room.

A giant wall of chocolate hit him in the nose.

ME WELL SPENT

1r. Nezzer thought his workers were just standing around. He didn't think they were sing their time the best way possible—saving the Chocolate Factory!

1 John's writings we learn that religious leaders were confused about how Jesus used is time too.

WHAT DOES THE BIBLE SAY?

John 2:1-11; 4:46-5:17

esus went to Jerusalem for a ewish feast. There, he passed by pool where a lot of disabled eople lay.

eople believed that at certain imes, angels would stir up the vater in the pool. If disabled people ould get into the pool while it was eing stirred, they believed they vould be healed.

ne poor guy had come to the pool very day for the past thirty-eight ears! He wanted badly to be ealed.

Iowever, the guy had no one who

could lift him into the water at the right time. So he asked Jesus if he would do that.

But Jesus did much more. "Get up! Pick up your mat and walk."

Instantly, the man was healed.

Healing people sounds like a pretty good use of time, doesn't it? But Jesus healed the crippled man on the Sabbath—a worship day. Some religious leaders believed you couldn't do ANY WORK on the Sabbath—not even heal people.

However, God will help people at any time on any day. After all, God is the King of kings!

BLE FACT:

he Mat Man—Some religious leaders were mad that Jesus told the isabled man to pick up his mat. They thought picking up a mat was work, /hich wasn't allowed on the Sabbath.

TOGETHER TIME

Turn off the television and spend time playing board games together. Or go for a hike, ride a bike, act out a Bible story, or help a neighbor. (You might even consider doing this every day for a week.

CUCUMBER CONNECTION

- What are some different ways you can make good use of your time?

- What do you spend too much time doing?

- What do you spend too little time doing?

THINK-LINK-ACT

THINK about ways in which you spend your time with God.

LINK that to specific ways you can work harder on doing things with and for God.

ACT on it by remembering to spend time with God on a regular basis. Record your progress on a calendar or in a journal.

"Whatever you do, work at it with all your heart" (Colossians 3:23a).
Lord, give me the strength to do your holy work.

votional - 39

IE HUNGRY MACHINE

I've got an idea," Mr. Nezzer said, popping a uarter into the vending machine for a soda. Let's make chocolate bunnies that never fill ou up. The more kids eat them, the hungrier hey get."

Parents will get mad if kids eat too much hocolate," said Larry the Cucumber.

That's OK, as long as they spend lots of money," Mr. Nezzer said, dropping in another quarter.

I don't know, Mr. Nezzer."

This machine keeps eating my quarters!" Mr. Nezzer yelled, putting in another one. Then nother. And another!

Looks like the vending machine is doing the ame thing to you that your chocolate bunny cheme would do to kids. The more quarters it ats, the hungrier it gets!"

Very funny!" Mr. Nezzer shouted, putting in ifty more quarters. "I give up. Maybe it is mean o create chocolate bunnies that make kids hun-rier. Forget the idea."

CLUNK! At very moment, a soda dropped out f the machine.

LIVING WATER

It was a dastardly plan—creating chocolate bunnies that make you feel even hungrie But that's how it is with a lot of things in life. The more we have, the more we want!

Jesus is different. All we need is Jesus in our lives. He satisfies us. He fills us up. Just ask the woman at the well.

WHAT DOES THE BIBLE SAY

John 4:1-38

Some strange things were happening at the well in the city of Sychar.

Jesus told a Samaritan woman that he would give her a drink of water. But he didn't have a bucket. So how could he give her water?

Jesus told her he could give her a special kind of water—LIVING WATER. If she drank this water, she would never be thirsty again. The woman was quite surprised!

But Jesus wasn't talking about real water. He was talking about himself. Jesus was trying to tell the woman that if she followed him, she would find joy forever.

We all look for happiness, just like thirsty person looks for water. We want happiness as badly as we wan water on a hot day. Only Jesus can make us truly happy.

If you saw someone dying of thirst you'd give him water. So open your eyes. All around us, people thirst for Jesus. Share the good news about Jesus. It's like giving a thirsty woman a cup of cool, clear water.

It's like giving her living water.

BIBLE FACT:

The Samaritan Woman—The woman at the well did many bad things in her past. But somehow Jesus knew all about it. This amazed her. She told her whole town about him.

OYFUL MENU

Create a restaurant menu. On one page, st delicious things that don't really fill s up. These things might make us appy for a short time. But they don't ive us lasting happiness. These are things like money, toys, popularity, chocolate, and so on.

On the second page of the menu, list the one thing that will make us joyful forever—Living Water. Write down ways that Jesus makes life better.

CUCUMBER CONNECTION

- How does following Jesus make us happy?
- What did Jesus mean by saying he could give the woman Living Water?
- How would you feel if Jesus offered you Living Water?

THINK-LINK-ACT

THINK about the things you can do to follow Jesus.

LINK those ideas to knowing that the good news is for everyone.

ACT on it by sharing the good news with a friend who doesn't know Jesus. Tell him or her how Jesus gives us eternal life.

he Lamb . . . will be their shepherd; he will lead them to springs of living water" evelation 7:17). Jesus, thank you for giving us living water. Help us share it with ople who thirst for happiness.

I WILL USE MY TIME TO SERVE OTHERS

MR. CHOCOLATE

Mr. Chocolate, the man who owned 20 chocolate factories, was coming to inspect Mr. Nezzer's Chocolate Factory.

"Oh no!" shouted Mr. Nezzer. "Someone left a candy wrapper on the factory floor. Someone's got to clean it up before Mr. Chocolate gets here."

But Mr. Nezzer was too important to pick up the wrapper himself.

Mr. Lunt didn't have time to pick up the wrapper.

Bob and Larry wouldn't pick up the wrapper. It wasn't their job.

NO ONE WOULD PICK UP THE WRAPPER!

Finally, an asparagus said he would pick it up. This made Mr. Nezzer very happy. He asked the asparagus to scrub the floor and polish the tanks while he was at it.

As the asparagus left, Mr. Lunt wandered into the room. "I see you just met Mr. Chocolate. Did he like our factory?"

"Huh? You mean . . . THAT asparagus was Mr. Chocolate!?"

"Of course," said Mr. Lunt. "Who did you think he was, boss?"

Mr. Nezzer didn't answer. He had just fainted.

ASH YOUR FEET BEFORE DINNER

Sometimes, we think we're too busy to serve others. We have more important things to do—like play video games or watch television.

But Jesus always took time to serve others.

WHAT DOES THE BIBLE SAY?

John 13:1-20

Jesus surprised his disciples one day when they came together for a special meal. He took out a bowl of water and started washing his disciples' feet!

Washing someone's feet at a meal might sound kind of strange. But it was very common in Bible days. Back then, roads were dusty. So when people arrived at your house, their feet were dusty too. Servants would often wash their feet. It was a dirty job, but someone had to do it.

Imagine how shocked the disciples were when Jesus started washing their feet. Wasn't he the Messiah? The King? Why would he do the job of a lowly servant?

In fact, Peter said he wouldn't let Jesus wash his feet. But Jesus answered, "Unless I wash you, you have no part with me."

So Peter allowed Jesus to wash his feet, and said, "Then Lord, not just my feet, but my hands and my head as well."

Jesus is King. Jesus is God. But he is also a servant. He takes the time to care for even our smallest need.

BLE FACT:

Dinner Is Served—During Jesus' time, the dining room table was very low to the floor. People did-n't really "sit" at the table. They leaned on a pillow on one elbow. This meant that people's head and feet were near each other. That's why having clean feet was important during meals.

FOOT WASHERS

Have a foot-washing race. Take turns taking off your shoes and socks and putting shaving cream on the bottom of your feet. Then use a squirt gun or spray bottle to wash off the shaving cream. Time each foot washer. See who can wash feet in the fastest amount of time.

CUCUMBER CONNECTION

- Why did Jesus wash his disciples' feet?
- What are other ways that Jesus served people?
- What are ways you can serve people?

THINK-LINK-ACT

THINK about several ways in which you can serve others that you may normally avoid.

LINK those ideas to the way in which Jesus served his disciples by washing their feet.

ACT on it by making a Servant's Time Sheet. Write down the ways you will serve people in the coming weeks. Then record how much tim you spent doing each one. Figure out new wa to serve in the weeks ahead.

"Even the Son of Man did not come to be served, but to serve [others]" (Mark 10:45a). Lord, help us to find the time to serve and love one another.

PART SIX

THE JOY CONNECTION

CONNECTING TO JOY BY LOOKING AT DAVID'S LIFE

The Joy Connection Verse

"You have made known to me the path of life;
you will fill me with joy in your
presence, with eternal pleasures
at your right hand."
(Psalm 16:11)

WELCOME TO MADAME BLUEBERRY'S TREE HOUSE

I'm so blue-hoo-hoo, blue-hoo-hoo, blue-hoo-hoo-HOO. I'm so blue I don't know what to do!

My name is Madame Blueberry, and I used to sing that song all of the time. Back then, I was a very blue berry. I was very sad, which is what feeling "blue" means. The good news is that I'm not as sad as I used to be. That's because I discovered God's joy.

God's joy is a special kind of happiness that helps us deal with sad things. We're going to learn a lot about God's joy in the next eight devotionals. We're also going to learn about David from the Old Testament.

David wrote a lot of "psalms," which are like poems that can be set to music. Some of David's psalms are about sad things. But many of the psalms are about David's joy.

So come on over to my tree house. Just take a left turn at the Stuff-Mart, an enormous store filled with—well, stuff! My butlers, Bob and Larry, will make you feel right at home.

While you're here, we might even get a visit from the Stuff-Mart salesmen. They'll probably try to sell you a giant air compressor to blow fruit flies off your dresser. Or would you rather have some bungee cords? You'll get to meet Mr. Gripe, who was once a very grouchy, old grape because he was so worried about having enough stuff, especially bungee cords!

Bungee! Bungee! Bungee-wungee-fungee! Here we go, bungee! Come on! Let's go!

GOD IS MY SOURCE OF JOY

THE SPIDER NIGHT

Larry, Bob, and Junior hiked up hills, through forests, and underneath raging waterfalls. They praised God for his wonderful creation. They were truly joyful.

That is, until they decided to sleep under the stars. In the middle of the night, Junior felt something on his nose. Something small and black.

Is it a spider? Junior thought, terrified.

A poisonous bug? Or maybe a scorpion?

Junior was afraid to call out for help for fear of startling the spider. The hours dragged by. Still, the bug wouldn't budge.

Will it hurt if it bites? Junior fretted. Junior never fell asleep. Finally . . .

The sun came up. "Say, Junior! Did you know you have a fuzzie on your nose?" Larry asked.

Overjoyed that it was only a fuzzie, Junior leaped up. "Thank you, God!" he shouted to heaven.

"Wow," Larry said to Bob. "Junior even praises God for fuzzballs."

"He must be a morning person," said Bob.

JOY TO THE WORLD!

God created an amazing world. There's a lot to be joyful about—even spiders and other critters.

Of all the people in the Bible, David was one of the most joyful. He certainly had his share of tough times. But he loved God so much he wrote many songs of praise.

WHAT DOES THE BIBLE SAY?

Psalm 24:1-2

David was a warrior, a king, a poet, and a singer. He fought giants. He led armies into battle. He played the harp. And he wrote many psalms—which are like prayers put to music.

You might even say he was the world's first rock star.

David also overflowed with joy— a special kind of happiness that comes from God. Just listen to David's words in Psalm 24:1-2:

"The earth is the LORD's, and every-thing in it, the world, and all who live in it; for he founded it upon the seas, and established it upon the waters."

David praised God for the world and everything in it! That's because God was David's source of joy! David drew his strength from God. David trusted God. David received God's love with all his heart. David turned his life over to God and knew that everything good in his life came from God! That's why David praised God for his joy all the time.

BIBLE FACT:

Bethlehem—David grew up in the little town of Bethlehem—the very same town where Jesus was later born.

ATURE HIKE

ake a nature hike. Go to a nearby orest or walk through your neighbor-hood. Look for all of the things to praise God for—the trees, the animals,

the birds. If the weather is bad, find ways to praise God indoors—for family, friends, good health, a home, and so on.

See if others can guess something you're looking at. Say, "I'm joyful about some-thing that is the color_____ (say its color)." Then let everyone guess.

CUCUMBER CONNECTION

• Read the Joy Connection Verse: Psalm 16:11. What is joy?

• How do you show joy?

• How does God help us to be joyful?

THINK-LINK-ACT

THINK about your attitude. Are you a joyful person?

LINK your joy to God. Remember that prais-ing God helps us to be joyful.

ACT on it by writing a psalm to God, which is like a poem of "thank yous." Praise him for things in your life.

Shout with joy to God, all the earth" (Psalm 66:1). God, we praise you for the wonderful works of your hand.

I FIND JOY IN WHOM GOD CREATED ME TO BE

WORM STORY

"I'm too short, and my voice sounds funny," muttered Junior as he walked along the path with Madame Blueberry.

"But God made you special," she said, stopping to show Junior a cocoon dangling from a branch. "Inside this cocoon is a caterpillar who may have felt just like you do. But inside is a beautiful butterfly, just waiting to get out."

"And your point is . . . ?"

"You may not think you're special on the *outside*. But you're special on the *inside*."

Right before their eyes, the cocoon split apart and out came the most amazing . . . EARTHWORM?

"You're right, lady!" the worm said. "Yesterday, I didn't think I was special. So I crawled into this used cocoon hoping to turn into a butterfly. But listening to you, now I know that God made me special the way I am—a worm."

The worm wandered off, muttering, "That's the last time I'm getting an extreme makeover."

HE PROPHET AND THE KING

You can't judge a worm by his slimy outside. You can't judge people by how they ook on the outside either. It's what's inside their heart that counts.

ust ask Samuel the prophet. When Samuel was looking for a new king, he had to ook deeper than skin.

WHAT DOES THE BIBLE SAY?

1 Samuel 16:1-13

od told the prophet Samuel it was ime for a new king to lead God's peo-ble. The current king was Saul, who was not being obedient to God.

So Samuel went to the town of Bethlehem o choose a new king. Samuel looked at ll the people in Bethlehem, but he kept his eye on the family of Jesse.

First, Samuel spotted Eliab, Jesse's old-est son. Eliab was tall and handsome, so Samuel figured he'd make a good king.

But God said to Samuel, "Do not con-sider how handsome or tall he is. I have not chosen him. Man looks at how someone appears on the outside. But I ook at what is in the heart."

Next, Jesse's son Abinadab walked in front of Samuel. But he just wasn't the one.

Then Jesse's son Shammah walked by. But he wasn't the right one, either.

In all, seven of Jesse's sons walked by Samuel. But none of them were king material.

"Are these the only sons you have?" Samuel asked. Jesse told him he had one other son—the youngest named David.

So David, who had been watching sheep, was brought before Samuel. HE WAS THE ONE.

David wasn't as old or as tall as the oth-ers. But he had a heart that loved God.

David didn't become king right away. For now, he would stay a shepherd. But God had chosen him, and he would be king when it was the right time.

BLE FACT:

The Harp Player—David went from being a shepherd to being King Saul's assistant. When Saul felt unhappy, David played his harp to make he king feel better.

FAMILY TALENT SHOW

Have a family talent show. Sing. Perform a stunt or skit. Read a story or poem aloud. Anything you can think of.

Then talk about our talents and how God makes each of us special.

CUCUMBER CONNECTION

- David had a heart for God. What does that mea
- Think about how people see you on the outside. What do they miss by just looking at your outside?
- How has God made you special? Name as many things as you can!

THINK-LINK-ACT

THINK about a time when you may not hav felt special.

LINK those times to what you have learned about God creating you special.

ACT on it by thanking God for who he created you to be!

"You created my inmost being; you knit me together in my mother's womb. I praise you because I am fearfully and wonderfully made" (Psalm 139:13–14). Maker of heaven and earth, I'm joyful that you made me.

I CAN FIND JOY EVEN IN TIMES OF TRIAL

HE GREAT TREE HOUSE CONTEST

During the annual Tree House Festival, kids came from all over to see who could build the biggest and best tree house.

Annie felt very small around the big Pickle brothers. To them she was just a little girl.

The Pickle brothers built their tree houses in the tallest of trees. But Annie built her tree house in just a tiny little tree, yet a sturdy one.

The night before the judging, a monstrous storm ripped through the forest, tearing most of the trees right out of the ground.

But Annie's tree remained strong and sturdy.

"How did this shrimpy tree stay standing?" muttered Peter Pickle.

"That tree is small above the ground, but its roots hold it deep in the soil," explained Madame Blueberry, the contest judge. Then she stuck a large blue ribbon on Annie's tree house.

Small is strong when your roots run deep.

GIANT PROBLEMS

It doesn't take a giant to do giant things. No matter how small we feel, God gives us strength—like the roots of a tree. And this strength brings joy, even when we're facing giant-sized problems.

David was small, but he was rooted in God. That made him big enough to face a giant.

WHAT DOES THE BIBLE SAY?

1 Samuel 17:1-50

Goliath was nine feet tall. Every day, this giant from the Philistine army challenged the Israelite soldiers to come out and fight. But the Israelite soldiers were too afraid to face this giant.

But David was not afraid. He knew God was with him. So David said, "I'll go out and fight him."

"The Lord saved me from the paw of the lion," David said. "And he'll save me from the powerful hand of this Philistine too."

So David picked out five smooth stones and faced the giant. Goliath couldn't believe he was fighting this shrimp. He charged at David, ready to swat him like a fly.

Acting quickly, David put a stone in his slingshot and hurled it at the charging giant. SMACK! The stone hit Goliath in the forehead, and the nine-foot giant crashed to the ground like a falling redwood.

David looked small. But he had God on his side. And God is bigger than any giant.

BIBLE FACT:

Champions—Sometimes, battles in Bible times were decided by "champions." Instead of entire armies fighting, each side sent out its strongest champion—like Goliath. God is our champion.

OTS

ok at trees in your backyard, your
eighborhood, or a forest. Pick out your
vorite tree.

Study the roots at the base of the tree.
Talk about how roots make trees strong.
Roots hold the tree in the ground and
keep it from being blown over in
storms. Food and water also reach the
tree through the roots. Talk about how
God makes us strong and how reading
the Bible is like "spiritual food."

CUCUMBER CONNECTION

• Why did David think he could face a giant?

• How did God help David?

• How did David feel joy amidst his giant
problems?

THINK-LINK-ACT

THINK about a giant problem you have had
—or could have in the future.

LINK that giant problem to God. God is much
bigger than any problem we will ever have!

ACT on it by reading the story of David and
Goliath in 1 Samuel 17. Then trust that
God will help you through your giant
problem.

Sovereign, LORD, my strong deliverer, who shields my head in the day of
attle" (Psalm 140:7). Lord and King, thank you for giving us joy, even
hen we face giant problems.

I FIND JOY IN BEING CONTENT

Devotional - 44

BUNGEE CORDS AND SEEDS

Mr. Gripe was a real grump, even on his birthday. He asked for lots of bungee cords, but no one gave him any. That made him even grumpier.

Instead, someone gave him a silly packet of tree seeds. Mr. Grump planted a seed, but when he checked it the next day, nothing had grown. That made him grumpier still!

Not content to wait for the trees to grow, Mr. Gripe dug up the seed and gave them all to Madame Blueberry. She planted and happily took care of them. Four years later she had several sturdy trees. But here's the best part—bungee cords grew on them just like fruit!

Madame Blueberry had so many bungee cords that she started her own company, Blueberry Bungee, Inc.

Mr. Gripe couldn't believe his eyes when he saw the bungee tree! So he passed right out! Too bad he didn't have a bungee cord to keep him from hitting the ground.

NG OF THE GRUMPS

f Mr. Gripe had been content with his gift and waited for the seeds to grow, he could ave had a million bungee cords.

ood things don't usually come easily and quickly. Like seeds, they take time. David new that. He knew he would have to wait until the time was right to become king of srael. So David was content and happy to wait. The current king wasn't.

WHAT DOES THE BIBLE SAY?

1 Samuel 26:1-25

ing Saul was one grumpy king. He was also jealous of David. In act, Saul took an army of three housand men and chased David nto the desert. He wanted to kill David to prevent him from becoming the new king of Israel.

One night, David snuck into Saul's amp. He found Saul asleep with a pear near his head. But David new that God would be angry if he ecame king by killing Saul. So David was content to wait for the Lord's time.

David took Saul's spear and water ug and snuck back to his own

camp. Then he called out to Saul's soldiers, "Why didn't you guard the king? He's your master, isn't he?"

David told Saul that he had snuck into the camp but didn't hurt him—even though he could have.

Saul felt bad when he realized that David spared his life, while he had been trying to kill David. So Saul decided to stop chasing David and head home.

But Saul never did learn to be content. He remained the king of the Grumps. It wasn't too long before he was chasing David again!

BLE FACT:

pear Crazy—King Saul once threw a spear at David while David was laying the harp trying to make King Saul feel calmer. Fortunately, it nissed. Talk about grumpy!

149

"SMILE, SAUL!"

Play "Smile, Saul!" Pick someone to be Saul, the angry king who doesn't smile. Have that person sit in a chair. Then another person tries to make "Saul" smile in any way possible. However, that person cannot touch Saul. In other words, no tickling allowed.

Take turns being Saul. Use a watch to see who can keep from smiling the longest.

CUCUMBER CONNECTION

- What does it mean to be content?
- What things do you have a hard time waiting for?
- In what ways can you learn to be more content?

THINK-LINK-ACT

THINK about a time that you were discontent and grumpy.

LINK that time to how God wants us to be patient and wait on his timing.

ACT on it by becoming a "Grump-Buster." Look up two psalms that lift your spirits. Write them on large pieces of cardboard. Post them around the house.

GOURD'S

"Wait for the LORD; be strong and take heart and wait for the LORD" (Psalm 27:14). LORD, help us to be happy when we have to wait. Fill us with your hope.

I FIND JOY IN BEING THANKFUL

HE BIG PRIZE

Mr. Gripe strolled into Stuff-Mart to buy new bungee cords. Suddenly lights flashed, confetti dropped, and a band started playing.

"Congratulations!" shouted the Stuff-Mart manager. "You're our ONE MILLIONTH CUSTOMER!"

"Really?" said Mr. Gripe. "Do I win anything? What do I get?"

"Drum roll please," said the manager. "For being the one millionth customer, you have won . . . A PRETTY BALLOON!"

Mr. Gripe's smile vanished. "A balloon?"

"A PRETTY balloon! Aren't you going to thank us?"

"For this cheap prize? Here, kid," Mr. Gripe said to a little girl. "Have a balloon."

"Oh thank you, thank you," beamed the little girl.

Suddenly lights flashed again and the band played.

"The little girl just said THANK YOU!" declared the Stuff-Mart manager. "Because you said THANK YOU, little girl, you've won the keys to A BRAND-NEW TREE HOUSE!"

Mr. Gripe fainted.

"You never learn, do you?"

151

THE THANKFUL KING

We may not always win prizes for being thankful. But we do feel a lot happier. David thanked God every chance he had. Maybe that's one reason God made him king.

WHAT DOES THE BIBLE SAY?

2 Samuel 7:18-19; Psalm 100:1-5

David waited 20 years to become king of Israel. But when the day finally came, he was SOOOOOOOOO happy that he couldn't stop thanking God.

He thanked God for taking him a long way from being a shepherd boy.

He thanked God for keeping the promise to make him king.

He thanked God for being great.

He thanked God for saving the nation of Israel.

He thanked God for leading the Israelites out of slavery.

David was a "thank-you champion." His heart overflowed with joy.

Finally, David ended with a prayer. He asked that God would bless his royal house forever. Little did he know that God would answer this prayer in an amazing way. The greatest king of all time would come from David's royal house.

That King would be Jesus—a descendant of the royal house of David.

Now that's something to be thankful about!

BIBLE FACT:

When the new King David brought the ark of the covenant to Jerusalem, he danced in front of everyone. His wife was mad about the dancing, but David couldn't hide his joy.

TUFF-MART CATALOG

The Stuff-Mart has a catalog of—well—stuff! Create your own Stuff-Mart catalog, but instead f trying to sell stuff, fill it with stuff that ou're thankful for! Start out with a game. Each erson or team should write down all the stuff hey can think of in five minutes. The longest list wins a prize—a thankful dance from the other team!

Finish your Stuff-Mart catalog by working on it every day for the next week . Every day each one of you picks out something or someone for whom you're thankful. Find a picture that represents what you're thankful for. Paste it into the catalog. Write down why you're thankful and dance for joy!

CUCUMBER CONNECTION

- What three things are you most thankful about?

- How does being thankful bring us joy?

- How can you show your thanks to others and to God?

THINK-LINK-ACT

THINK about someone you really need to thank.

LINK it to the lesson that a thankful heart is a happy heart.

ACT on it by writing a thank-you note to that person.

My heart leaps for joy and I will give thanks to him in song" (Psalm 28:7). Thank you, God, for loving us. Let us sing your name forever and ever.

I FIND JOY IN BEING KIND

THE FOREST FLOOD

Mr. Gripe was mad at Madame Blueberry because she had a Bungee Tree and he didn't. So he decided to run for mayor and a build a highway right through her tree house!

That's when it started to rain. It poured so hard that the nearby river overflowed. It was a FLOOD!

"Help!" someone shouted.

Peeking out of her tree house, Madame Blueberry saw Mr. Gripe clinging to a piece of wood in the swirling floodwater!

"Quick! We've got to save him!" she said.

"Why?" asked her butler, Bob.

"Because God wants us to show kindness to others, no matter who it is," she said, looking for some way to help him.

"The bungee cords!" Bob shouted.

It was the perfect solution.

d Connection:

HE KING OF KINDNESS

Madame Blueberry surprised her butler, Bob, when she showed kindness to Mr. Gripe, even though he was trying to destroy her home. That's because God wants us to show kindness to others whether that person is nice to you or not.

David surprised people when he showed kindness in a most unexpected way.

2 Samuel 9:1-13

ing Saul's grandson, Mephibosheth, was crippled and could not use his feet. His father (Jonathan) and grandfather (King Saul) were killed in a great battle. Mephibosheth, worried that the new king would try to kill him. Back then, when new kings took over, they often killed the old king's family. So Mephibosheth hid.

But David had Mephibosheth found and brought to his palace. Mephibosheth was probably certain that David was going to kill him at this point. Instead, David treated him as if he were his very own son.

David was the new king, and he was different. "For I will surely show you kindness for the sake of your father Jonathan," David told him.

Because of David's kindness, he showed kindness to Mephibosheth. David gave him all of the money that had belonged to the old king, Saul. He even let Mephibosheth eat at his dinner table regularly.

Mephibosheth couldn't run and jump. But inside, his heart must've been jumping for joy!

IBLE FACT:

The Injury—When Mephibosheth's family was killed, his nurse took him and fled. But the nurse fell down while carrying him. That's how his feet were hurt (2 Samuel 4:4).

Family Fun Connection:
SURPRISE!

Write down something nice about each person in your family. (Help little ones by asking them to tell you what to write.) Tape a candy kiss or some type of treat, to the papers and hide them around the room. Have fun looking for and finding your treats of kindness!

Just like David surprised Mephibosheth with his kindness, find a way to surprise each other with kindness this week. Put names of family members in a hat. Draw a name out of the hat and surprise the person with kindness. But don't tell whose name you drew. It's a surprise!

CUCUMBER CONNECTION

• How do you feel when someone shows kindness to you?

• How does being kind to others give us joy?

• Why does God want us to show kindness to everyone, regardless of who they are?

THINK-LINK-ACT

THINK about the way you treat others.

LINK that to knowing that kindness makes people feel joy!

ACT on it by making this Kindness Week. Pick a special, kind thing to do for someone every day of the week. It could be doing a chore. Or making them something. I'll feel happy too!

"The LORD is gracious and righteous; our God is full of compassion" (Psalm 116:5). Lord, help us to show kindness in surprising ways.

I FIND JOY IN WALKING WITH GOD

PACKED HOUSE

Larry returned from the Stuff-Mart with dishes and sheets and toys and toasters! Later he returned with a new bicycle, pajamas, and a ceiling fan for every room. "I'll be back later!" he said. "I'm walking with God, and it feels GREAT!"

"You're packing the house with stuff!" Madame Blueberry scolded.

"David walked joyfully with God and sang praises to him!" Larry said. "So I'm joyfully walking back and forth from the Stuff-Mart praising God for all this stuff!"

"Walking with God means living the way God wants you to, not buying more stuff," Madame Blueberry explained.

"OK, Got it!" Larry said, heading out again.

"Where are you going now?"

"Back to the Stuff-Mart. I promised the manager I'd be back to buy some rose bushes."

"But Larry, walking with God doesn't mean filling our lives with more stuff!"

"No, but it does mean keeping our promises!" he said, as he headed out the door with a whistle.

THE RESCUER

In one of the greatest songs in the Bible, David rejoices and called the Lord "my place of safety." He said God reaches out to us when troubles wash over us like a "destroying flood."

As Madame Blueberry was trying to teach Larry, the Lord reaches out with love—not more stuff.

WHAT DOES THE BIBLE SAY?

2 Samuel 22:1-51

David had a joyful heart as he walked with God and sang praises to him. He looked at the earth and the sky, he saw so many things that brought him joy, because they reminded him of how great and wonderful God is.

But David went through tough times too. He was chased by King Saul. His son, Absalom, was murdered. His armies constantly battled the Philistines. But even in times of trouble, David walked with God.

David sang praises to God rejoicing about all the wonder of what he did! And David sang praises to God during times of hardship, because he knew that God would always give him strength to get through it.

In one of David's most famous songs in 2 Samuel 22, he sang that God was his STRENGTH. "The LORD is my rock, my fortress and my deliverer," He is the one who saves me." (v.2)

God was also his RESCUER. "He reached down from on high and took hold of me; He drew me out of deep waters." (v.17)

God was his LIGHT. "You are my lamp, O LORD; the Lord turns my darkness into light." (v.29)

God was his PROTECTOR. "He is a shield for all who take refuge in him." (v.31)

God was his FAITHFUL FRIEND. "To the faithful you show yourself faithful." (v.26)

In short, God was the joy of David's life. And when we walk with God, we'll have a joyful heart too.

BIBLE FACT:

David's son Absalom was a rebel. He tried to kick David out as king. But even with these troubles, David still found a way to be joyful.

NG ALONG

avid sang songs to God all of the time.
lave a family "Sing along to God" time.
ach person picks out their favorite

Christian song (including Christmas songs) and everyone sings the song together. If you're a musical family, play instruments together too. Praise God!

CUCUMBER CONNECTION

- What does it mean to "walk with God"?
- How can you find ways to better walk with God?
- How can you tell when someone is walking with God?

THINK-LINK-ACT

THINK about an area of your life in which you need to walk closer with God.

LINK all of God's blessings in our lives to the joy they give us.

ACT on it by walking with God, remembering him every day, and thanking him for his blessings to you.

he LORD lives! Praise be to my Rock! Exalted be God, the Rock, my Savior!"
2 Samuel 22:47). Lord, thank you for being my strength, my
escuer, my light, my protector, and my faithful friend.

Devotional - 48

GROUCHY TO GLAD

Madame Blueberry was hosting the annual Bungee Olympics! Everyone was looking forward to it—everyone except Mr. Gripe. He was still grouchy because he never got a bungee of his own, so he couldn't participate in the Bungee Olympics.

When the day arrived, Mr. Gripe watched Madame Blueberry host the games: bungee jumping, bungee dashes, bungee skiing, and bungee swimming.

Awards were given, and the crowds went wild with joy. Everyone was celebrating. Everyone except Mr. Gripe. After everyone went home, Madame Blueberry noticed that Mr. Gripe was sitting alone in the stadium.

"I could really use someone to take care of my bungee trees and host the Bungee Olympics for me next year. It's getting a bit too much for me," she told him.

Mr. Gripe looked up and smiled. From that day on they became good friends. In fact, Mr. Gripe wasn't grouchy anymore either. His life was filled with joy thanks to a very joyful blueberry.

HARE THE JOY

Madame Blueberry and Mr. Gripe had good reason to praise God. They had joyful hearts because of Madame Blueberry's willingness to share in her joy.

When we're joyful, our happiness sometimes spills out and makes others happy too. So splash a little joy around. David did.

WHAT DOES THE BIBLE SAY?

Palm 145

avid wrote many songs in the book of Psalms. He talked about things that made him mad, sad, afraid, and happy. He also praised God over and over.

n Psalm 145, David said that God was GREAT: "no one can fathom his greatness." (v.3)

Also, he said God is KIND AND TENDER: "slow to anger and rich n love." (v.8)

God is GOOD TO ALL. "He has compassion on all he has made." (v.9)

God is FAITHFUL. "[He] lifts up all who are bowed down." (v.14)

God is RIGHT in everything he does. "The LORD is near to all who call on him in truth." (v.18)

When we're excited by good news, we want to run out and tell everyone. That's how David felt about God. He wanted to shout his joy from the rooftops!

David shared his joy in the Lord when he wrote psalms. That's so that we could hear his joy and be touched by it too!

BLE FACT:

Some psalms were written for people to sing alone. But some psalms were for groups. In fact, soldiers sometimes sang psalms while marching nto battle.

SPREAD THE JOY!

Play games, like tag. If it's warm, do fun things with water. Have kids use a squirt bottle to knock a paper cup from a parent's head. Toss water balloons high in the air and let the kids try to catch them. (If you're in a park, be sure to pick up the broken balloons.)

If it's bad weather outside, have a picnic on your living room floor. Play board games together. Tell jokes and have a giggling contest. Whatever you do together, spread the joy!

CUCUMBER CONNECTION

• Do you feel joy in the Lord?

• Why did David write psalms?

• How can you share your joy in the Lord with others?

THINK-LINK-ACT

THINK about someone who needs to feel more joyful.

LINK that to ways that you feel joyful. How can you share your joy with them?

ACT on it by inviting that person to your house for fun and ice cream!

"All you have made will praise you, O LORD; your saints will extol you. They will tell of the glory of your kingdom," (Psalm 145:10–11a). Lord, we praise you for being good, kind, faithful, and right in everything you do.

PART SEVEN

HOLIDAY LESSONS

CONNECTING TO GOD AT NEW YEAR'S, EASTER, THANKSGIVING, AND CHRISTMAS

The Holiday Verse

"Come near to God and he
will come near to you."
(James 4:8)

HAPPY HOLIDAYS!

Ho! Ho! Away we go! With rosy cheeks and hearts a-glowing. Hey! Hey! My favorite day! It makes me want to cheer!

This is Larry the Cucumber again, and oh my do I have a lot of favorite days in the year. I'm very big on Lips Appreciation Day, which falls on March 16. And I can't wait for Talk Like a Pirate Day every September 19.

We're going to end this devotional with some fun devotionals for my four favorite days of all: New Year's, Easter, Thanksgiving, and Christmas.

For New Year's, we're going back to Snoodleburg to learn all about starting the new year out . . . ah . . . new!

For Easter, we'll check out Mr. Nezzer's Easter Egg Factory. Yep, he's the brother of Mr. Nezzer who runs the Chocolate Factory! This Mr. Nezzer learned a very important lesson about the real meaning of Easter. You'll have a great time!

For Thanksgiving, we'll drop in on Madame Blueberry's Tree House. She's still a very thankful blueberry, so we thought it was a good place to go to celebrate thankfulness!

We'll wrap it all up with a traditional Christmas with Bob and me. (Get it? *Wrap it up.* Christmas presents—wrapping paper!) Anyway, for Christmas we'll be focusing on the reason we have Christmas—Jesus!

It's been fun spending time with you all year long. So if you're ever in VeggieTown, drop by any time. Until then, remember that GOD MADE YOU, AND HE LOVES YOU VERY MUCH!

Hey Bob! What are you getting me for National Sea Monkey Day on May 16?

HAPPY NEW YEAR!

Devotional - 49

NO MESS-UPS ALLOWED

On New Year's Eve at the Snoodlburg Art and Waffle School the school's headmaster, Noodles McCloud, announced the traditional New Year's rule.

"This year," said Mr. McCloud, "Every artist and waffle-maker must promise that they WILL NEVER MESS UP when they're drawing, painting, or cooking waffles!"

Never mess up? How was that possible?

For the next month, every artist drew with care. If a line was crooked, they couldn't erase. No mess-ups allowed.

If they spilled a can of paint on their picture, they couldn't start over. No mess-ups allowed.

If their waffle came out burnt, they had to eat it. No mess-ups allowed.

When the Creator who lived on Mt. Ginchez found out about this rule, he wasn't too pleased. So he went to Noodles McCloud, and here's what he said:

No one is perfect. And that includes you.
So tear up that rule. I've got one that's new.
When you mess up, Mr. Noodles McCloud,
Just make a new start. THAT'S all that's allowed.

IN THE BEGINNING

The New Year is a fresh start. A new beginning. It's also a good time to remember that our Lord is a God of new beginnings.

Whenever we mess up, all we have to do is ask and God is always there to forgive us. He gives us second chances. It's as if God crumples up our list of sins and mistakes and tosses them in the wastebasket. He makes us a New Creation.

WHAT DOES THE BIBLE SAY?

Genesis 1:1-31

From the beginning, God has been in the new creation business.

On the first day of Creation, God made light. He said, "Let there be light" and it happened.

On the second day, God created the sky.

On the third day, God created the land and the oceans. Then the land grew plants, and he said it was good.

On the fourth day, God created the sun and the moon. And it was good.

On the fifth day, God created birds and creatures of the ocean. And it was good.

On the sixth day, God created animals. He also created man and woman. And it was VERY good.

The first man and the first woman were very good, but they weren't perfect. They disobeyed God and brought sin into the world. But did God give up on people? No way. Our Lord is a God who knows we will mess up, and is ready to give us a fresh start.

So Happy New Year! And Happy New Beginnings!

BIBLE FACT:

"Create" means "to make something brand new."

EFRIGERATOR ART

Create a Refrigerator Art Gallery. Draw and color pictures of the seven days of creation. Attach them to your refrigerator with magnets. And if you mess up, don't worry. You can always start again.

CUCUMBER CONNECTION

• When you mess up, how do you feel?

• When you are forgiven, how do you feel?

• What were your favorite memories of the past year?

THINK-LINK-ACT

THINK about things you'd like to start over.

LINK those desires to knowing that when things go wrong, God will forgive us and create a new start for us.

ACT on it by writing a New Year's prayer—something you'd like to pray for throughout the year. Put it in an envelope and don't open it until next New Year's.

Create in me a pure heart, O God, and renew a steadfast spirit within me" (Psalm 51:10). Lord, thank you for making everything new and fresh—including my heart.

HAPPY EASTER!

EASTER FOREVER

"Plastic is where it's at!" declared Mr. Nezzer at the Easter Trade Show. "Plastic lasts forever! Not like real eggs, which break or rot!"

To prove it, Mr. Nezzer placed a plastic Easter egg next to a real egg. "Not only can real eggs break, but they can't be painted by machines . . ."

At that very moment, the real egg wobbled and shook and started to crack. Then out peeped a little baby chick.

"Oooooooooooooooooooh," said the crowd, gathering around the little chick.

"Don't you want to hear more about my plastic eggs?" said Mr. Nezzer.

"Your plastic eggs can't LIVE forever," said one man. "This chick is ALIVE!"

Mr. Nezzer had to admit that new life is exciting. After all, new life is what Easter is all about.

"The chick *is* cute," he said, picking up the bird. When he took a seat, he accidentally sat on his plastic egg, squashing it flat. But no one noticed—not even Mr. Nezzer.

APPY ENDINGS

When the baby chick came out of its shell, new life was born.

When Jesus came out of the tomb, his disciples discovered that Jesus was alive!

New life brings hope. Hope is when we know that no matter what happens in life, God will take care of us. Jesus gives us this hope.

WHAT DOES THE BIBLE SAY?

Luke 23-24:12

When Jesus was arrested, he was taken before Pilate, the Roman leader. Pilate didn't think Jesus had done anything to be punished for. But the people who hated Jesus shouted, "Crucify him!" They had hate, not hope.

So Pilate gave in and decided to have Jesus killed. Things were looking completely hopeless!

Jesus was forced to carry a huge, heavy cross to a mountain called the Skull. There, Roman soldiers nailed him to the cross and hung him between two other prisoners.

One of the prisoners made fun of Jesus. But the other prisoner said,

"This man has done nothing wrong." Then he turned to Jesus and asked Jesus to remember him so he could go to heaven. That prisoner had hope, not hate.

"Today, you will be with me in paradise," Jesus answered.

After a terrible, painful time on the cross, Jesus died. But three days later, Jesus rose from the dead. He was alive! He had defeated death.

Jesus showed that God has a happy ending for everyone who follows him. When you love and follow Jesus then death really isn't an ending— only a wonderful beginning.

BLE FACT:

Jesus was killed by what's called a "crucifixion." His hands and feet were nailed to a wooden cross and he couldn't breathe. But Jesus forgave the people who did this to him.

EGG HUNT

Put extra meaning in your Easter egg hunt. Give everyone a large plastic egg that can be opened. Ask each person to find something that shows the meaning of Easter to them. Then put it in the egg. Have these eggs be part of the hun[t]

After the egg hunt, open the plastic eggs. Try to guess who came up with each Easter symbol. Talk about what th[e] symbols mean.

CUCUMBER CONNECTION

- Why did Jesus die for us?
- Why did he rise from the dead?
- How does this make you feel?

THINK-LINK-ACT

THINK about what it would feel like if you didn't have faith in Jesus.

LINK that to the hope we are given in the birth, death, and resurrection of Jesus!

ACT on it by taking time to celebrate Jesus— the real reason for Easter, and share that joy with a friend!

"[Jesus] is not here; he has risen!" (Luke 24:6a). Jesus, thank you for defeating death and giving us all hope.

HAPPY THANKSGIVING!

HE FLYING TURKEY

One year Larry the Butler accidentally destroyed Madame Blueberry's Thanksgiving turkey, so they ordered out Chinese.

"This year, I'm being extra careful," Larry said. "This year, I'm—Woops!"

Larry dropped a dinner roll, which hit a fork, which shot across the room and knocked down a vase, which hit a bowling ball, which rolled across the floor, which shattered one of the table legs. The table fell and the turkey slid out the window.

Below the tree house was a poor family thankful for just one slice of pie.

"Thank you, God, for our little piece of pie and for—"

WHOMP!

Madame Blueberry's turkey landed squarely on their table.

"Thank you, God!" they shouted.

Madame Blueberry looked down from her tree house. "Order me egg rolls this year," she said with a smile.

"I'm already on it," said Larry, picking up the phone.

THANKS FOR EVERYTHING!

The secret in life is to be thankful for what you have—just like the poor family who had only one slice of pie for Thanksgiving.

A thankful heart is a happy heart. It's also a giving heart.

WHAT DOES THE BIBLE SAY?

Mark 12:41-44

One day, Jesus sat down across from the temple. He watched different people give their offering—money given for others.

Many rich people came by and put huge amounts of money in the offering box. But then a curious thing happened. A widow, a poor woman whose husband had died, came walking by.

The widow put two small copper coins in the offering box. Those two coins weren't even worth as much as a single penny!

Jesus told his disciples that the poor widow put in more money than all of the rich people. But how could that be?

Jesus said the rich people gave a lot but they gave only a small amount of what they owned. That poor widow gave everything she owned. Every last coin.

The widow had little, but she was thankful for what she had to give. She was thankful for EVERYTHING.

BIBLE FACT:

The temple collection boxes were called "the trumpets." There were thirteen of them, and they were shaped a bit like . . . trumpets.

APPY HEARTS

Give each family member five pennies. Then go around and take turns naming something thankful. If you cannot say something thankful within three seconds of your turn, you must forfeit a penny to the person on your right. At the end of your game time, whoever has the most pennies is the person with the happiest heart for the day!

CUCUMBER CONNECTION

• Why was Madame Blueberry thankful that her turkey landed on the poor family's table?

• How did the widow give more money than the rich people?

• How does being thankful make you happy?

THINK-LINK-ACT

THINK about ways you can show God and others that you are thankful.

LINK that to remembering that a thankful heart is a happy heart.

ACT on it by making a chart for your refrigerator. Have every person in the family note one thing they are thankful for every day for one week. Say thanks to God for these things during your dinner prayer each night.

ive thanks to the LORD, for he is good; his love endures forever" Psalm 118:1). Lord, THANK YOU for what we have. You're so good.

MERRY CHRISTMAS!

THE TWO WISE MEN

"I can't wait to see what you got me!" Larry said to Bob, ripping into his Christmas gift. "You got me a . . . uh . . . *hairbrush?*"

"You're always singing that song, 'Oh Where Is My Hairbrush?'" said Bob. "So I got you a solid gold hairbrush. I even had your initials put on it."

"But I don't have any hair," Larry said, quite disappointed.

Next, Bob excitedly opened the gift from Larry. It was a pair of mittens with built-in solar-powered heaters. Bob's name was monogrammed on it!

"But Larry, I don't have any hands," said Bob.

"Oh. Good point."

Larry and Bob looked very sad. They couldn't return the gifts because their names were on them. But then it dawned on them. Christmas was about GIVING, not getting.

They had both spent a lot of time shopping for those presents. It showed they cared.

Excited once again, they ripped into the rest of their presents.

"Toenail clippers?"

"I'll trade you for hand lotion."

"Okay!"

D'S CHRISTMAS PRESENT

ike Bob and Larry's Christmas, the very first Christmas wasn't perfect either. Lots
f things went wrong for Mary and Joseph. But it was still the greatest Christmas of
hem all.

WHAT DOES THE BIBLE SAY?

Luke 2:1-20

oseph and Mary had to travel all
he way to Bethlehem to put their
ame on a Roman list. It was the
ule.

he journey was rough because
Mary was pregnant. In fact, when
hey reached Bethlehem, it was
ime for Mary to have her baby. But
when they went to the inn, they
ound it packed to the rafters with
eople.

o Mary and Joseph had to sleep in
he stable with animals. In this
lark, stinky place, Mary gave birth
o the King of the world. Jesus was
orn!

Meanwhile, some shepherds were
out in the field with their flocks of
sheep when an angel appeared. The
angel said that the Savior had been
born. Then a whole bunch of angels
started singing, which was a pretty
good clue that something big had
just happened. So the shepherds
went to the stable, where they
found the baby Jesus.

On that first Christmas, none of the
shepherds got toys or bicycles or
video games. But everyone knew
deep down they had been given the
greatest Gift of all.

God had given himself.

BLE FACT:

he stables in Bethlehem were usually caves, not buildings. Jesus was
orn in a cave, and he rose from the dead in a cave.

A CHRISTMAS BOOK

Act out the Christmas story using stuff around the house for costumes. Take photographs of different scenes that you act out: the trip to Bethlehem, the innkeeper, the birth in the stable, the angels, the shepherds and the three kings. When you get the photos printed make them into a Christmas book.

CUCUMBER CONNECTION

- What is your favorite Christmas present of all time?
- What is the best Christmas present that you ever gave?
- What is the best thing you've ever been given by God?

THINK-LINK-ACT

THINK about what it's like to get Christmas gifts.

LINK that to remembering that it's more joyful to give than get.

ACT on it by writing a Christmas giving list. Write down things you want to give—but not just material things. Write down things like "sharing with my sister" or "helping my dad."

"I bring you good news of great joy that will be for all the people. Today in the town of David a Savior has been born to you; he is Christ the Lord" (Luke 2:10b–11). Thank you, Lord, for the greatest Christmas present of all—your Son, our King.